Last of the Best

A memoir

Sophie Randell

Published by Forty Nine Press
3639 Wild Orchid Court
Wake Forest, NC 27587
emily.bellflower@gmail.com

ISBN: 9-781530-978915

"Oh that my words were now written!
Oh that they were printed in a book!
That they were graven with an iron pen and lead
in the rock forever!"
Job 19:23-24 KJV

Dedicated to all the girls who entered the three year diploma nursing schools and came out again forever changed. Sisters all.

When sisters stand shoulder to shoulder
who stands a chance against us?

Pam Brown

The stories you are about to read are true, the names have been changed to protect the innocent and the guilty.

Table of Contents:

First Year – September 1956- September 1957

Second Year – September 1957 – September 1958

Table of Contents (continued)   <u>Page</u>

Third Year – September 1958- September 1959

Prologue

It is the year of Our Lord 2014, can it be possible that over fifty years have passed since we graduated from nursing school? Nursing schools dotted the landscape all over the country in those days and we belonged to that unique group of health providers, diploma school nurses.

Approximately nine of us who still live locally have been getting together almost every month for lunch, at restaurants, picnic areas or in each other's homes since graduation. In doing so we have kept alive the memories of those days when we lived with one another for three very long years in what would be considered today very unusual circumstances. After all, hadn't we been fellow slaves, recipients of a supposedly character building business that had its roots in the Florence Nightingale Pledge, preparing young uninformed, naive girls to tend the sick?

Somewhere between Florence Nightingale and the mid twentieth century, "herding" became the accepted norm. Young women who entered nursing schools were placed in buildings called nurses' residences with strict rules to govern behavior and facilitate learning. Teams of nursing instructors were hired. The basic philosophy was that strict "boot camp" like methods would be applied to turn silly young ladies into proper, respected, dedicated sick care providers who would also exhibit persons' of high moral character in their personal private lives.

This philosophy was greatly tested in September 1956, when the class of September 1959 entered what was then named the Wayside School of Nursing. It was affiliated with Wayside Hospital located in an eastern industrial city.

In the 1950's the majority of young high school graduates sought employment at several industrial complexes in the area and never pursued further education. So "going into nursing" was venturing outside of the box so to speak.

During the many years of lunching together we continued to keep alive memories of our training days by sharing our personal and collective experiences. But who would know about those unique days? So it was decided, let us record it all into a book. But what format would we use? Should it contain just a collection of memories or individualized orderly personal accounts? We agreed, each one would contribute by sharing some of her own special unique experiences.

So here are our stories written to preserve a time that would never be again, collected from nine written into a book by one.

Jill Lee – January 2014

The cast of contributors – in alphabetical order, of course.

Grace Carlson – a city girl, homecoming queen, precise, neat as a pin, bright, a forever friend and loves pretty clothes, shoes and hats.

Reva Flanagan – small town girl, unique, witty, talented, fair minded, observant, faithful friend and loves to clean and decorate.

Feona Hartman - bright, fun loving, good humored, contagious laugher, boon companion and loves to entertain.

Katie Hatter – country girl, hard working, clear sighted, dedicated to tasks, helpful friend and loves to collect and organize.

Lindsay Hinkle – true home bound country girl, beautiful, whimsical, perfectionist and loves to be with family.

Jill Lee - small town girl, shy, self conscious, fainter, loyal, naive, dedicated and loves to travel under the radar.

Rachael Lucas – city girl with small town roots, trustworthy, accomplished, quiet, steady companion and loves family life.

Pauline Macy - city girl, hard worker, responsible, quick witted, trusted friend, and loves to help other people.

Josephine (Jo Jo) Walker – country girl, tomboy, curious, keen, striver, friendly, determined and loves to dream about wearing a white uniform.

WAYSIDE HOSPITAL SCHOOL OF NURSING
JULY 12, 1956

Dear Student Applicant:

In preparing to come into the School of Nursing, we suggest that you limit your clothing to essentials. There is very limited space available in the Nurses Residence. (Do not bring a trunk.)

Laundry is limited to uniforms and plain cotton wear.

Time lost through illness is made up at the end of the course, also absence.

Passing grade of School is 75%.

TUITION: First year $220.00. $10.00 of this amount is payable when returning Acceptance blank, balance of $210.00 payable on day of admission to School. Second year tuition fee $65.00, payable on or before the beginning of the second year (September).

You will need the following articles:

1. Watch with a second hand.
2. Fountain pen, pencil, eraser.
3. Two plain laundry bags with name – unbleached muslin will be satisfactory.
4. Umbrella and overshoes to fit duty shoes.
5. Plain white orthopedic to fit duty shoes.
6. Approximately 3 pairs white stockings.
7. Plain cotton slips.
8. All articles of clothing to be plainly marked.
9. Two 8 x 11 note books, plain and ruled paper.
10. An alarm clock.
11. Shoe bag.
12. Rubber apron for laboratory work. (This apron can be purchased here at the School on day of admission - $.65).

WAYSIDE HOSPITAL SCHOOL OF NURSING

Charlotte W. Rivers.

(Mrs.) Charlotte W. Rivers, R.N.
Director of Nurses

FIRST YEAR

September 1956 – September 1957

Chapter 1

The First Day of the Rest of My Life
Jill

I was born at home in a small town twenty miles from the Wayside Hospital Nursing School. Growing up, I never even wanted to be a nurse. But in the 1950s there were few choices for women. It was either business school, teaching or nursing. After I had worked summers for two years in a Main Street 5&10 cent store at 25 cents an hour (later raised to 40 cents), my Dad began to go on and on about how I could never expect more unless I had an education in some field. Business school was out. I failed shorthand in school; and who would want to stand up and teach rooms filled with nasty, noisy and unruly kids? So nursing it was. I was sure I could handle the blood thing since I couldn't recall ever feeling sick when once in a while I cut myself or witnessed someone with a bloody nose. Ignorant, I was indeed, of the whole medical world. So as a "lamb to the slaughter is dumb," I applied and was accepted pending some improvement on the math part of the entry test. For some unknown reason I did well the second time and I was "in" or should I say "out" of all that represented a normal life for young girls in their late teens.

The nurses' home is shaped like a large rectangle with doors at front, back and both ends. There are three stories and a completed basement. Having many windows and constructed of yellow brick, it stands like an armed fort on a hill. All rooms on the second and third floors are small rooms for two. On each end, there are two larger rooms, furnished for four. In the center towards the back is a wash room with five sinks, four toilets, two showers and one bath tub. There are beds enough on each floor for forty girls. The first floor has a lobby in the center and rooms down both ends. At the end of the right corridor is the housemother's quarters. The basement includes a small lounge, a utility room, furnace room, library, a few small classrooms and a large common room with a kitchen tucked away in one corner. This room is used for some classes and other activities. It also houses an upright piano and a stereo with a stack of records.

The two top floors have an iron rail balcony with some rope lines to hang laundry. The grounds surrounding the building are lovely, full of old trees and some late fall blooming flowers. A tennis court on the left side of the place is in a rather battered condition.

This façade stared back at me when Dad dropped me off at curbside and I trudged up the long front walk with shaking knees on that first day. Small pinpricks of anxiety stuck me between heart and head. Did I look as anxious as I felt? I silently assured myself, "Really, Jill get a hold of yourself. There isn't a firing squad ahead just a lobby for signing in. Surely people will be kind and helpful getting you settled."

Through the doors I went and off to the right was a desk with a rather severe looking person behind it (so much for kind and helpful). "Name please," she barked. "J-J-Jill L-Lee," I stuttered. "Set your things down and sign in and who is your roommate?"

Roommate? I was at a loss for a reply. Five girls in my high school class were coming here. I knew their names but none were close friends. No doubt they already had roommates. However, I did slightly know one girl, a year ahead of me in high school, who was entering this year. So I spurted out her name "Reva Flanagan."

"Alright, take your things, go to the end of the hall and take the stairs to the third floor, Room 304", she announced.

I stumbled off wondering what Reva would think. Maybe she already had a roommate. What then would I do? Pushing my shabby suitcase (it belonged to my grandmother) and the rather large cardboard box (shoes and boots) into room 304, I looked around; one rather small window, a dresser with four drawers and a mirror, bunk beds, a desk, two chairs and on the left one very small closet. Stark and prison-like, bare and unwelcoming, my spirits sank. How could such a beautiful September day become so alarmingly dismal? I sat down on one of the uncomfortable chairs and wiped away a few tears. This wouldn't do, I must be more positive.

Just then I heard a shuffle and in walked Reva. Did the sun just burst in through that one dirty window or was it her beautiful welcoming smile that changed everything? Here was my roommate who apparently had no prearranged assignment; she had flaming red hair, lovely pale skin with freckles here and there, perfect teeth and no evidence of anxiety anywhere. All would surely be well. She flopped down on the bottom bunk, took a deep breath and said "You must take the top one. I'm desperately afraid of high places." Just a few minutes with her and somehow I knew, here was a friend that would be mine forever.

Under her expert directions, we split up the space, two drawers each, and one half of the closet. The limited space was adequate as neither of us had an over abundance of clothes or personal items. She had an alarm clock with a radio, for Pete's sake! (So alarms and the top 100 tunes would become an intricate part of our lives.) "As soon as possible," she said, "we must do something about this awful room, even a twig from a tree would help. I must tell mother we need at least one colorful rug to cover this nasty brown floor, and oh the walls, what a horrid green color they are! Whoever was the interior decorator, he or she should be shot." I had nothing to add but agreed completely. Where did they keep the guns? We laughed and talked and laughed some more.

So what was next on the schedule in this nasty place and when would they feed us? We looked over the papers previously mailed to us. Dinner, 5 p.m. at the hospital dining area (where was that?) and then on to orientation at the large classroom in the basement at 6 p.m. We would just cross over to the hospital and follow our noses for dinner and then follow the other 44 girls to the large classroom. So off we went. Yes, my roommate and I.

Chapter 2
Rules for the Unruly
Feona

Orientation at 6 p.m. and here we are looking around the room at all the girls, all sizes and shapes, all young and almost all looking very anxious. I slid in with Ava, my roommate, to two empty chairs in the third row. It is a little like church, all the back chairs are taken and no one is sitting in the front row. Miss Walls is telling us to open up our nursing handbooks. She apparently is the Educational Director. Not very tall with white hair and glasses, dressed in a nurse's uniform, she looks rather old, at least fifty. Sitting behind her is an even older looking gray haired lady in street clothes. Miss Walls introduced her to us as the resident Housemother, Mrs. Stone. Mrs. Stone is looking us over with suspicious eyes, like she has been here before and is equipped and ready for battle. No welcoming comments are forthcoming from her. Well, I didn't come from a wimpy town but a blue collar no nonsense place. My father is a tough conductor on the railroad and my mother is not one to stand down for anyone. This housemother appears to be quite the challenge that must be met with vim and vigor. I am ready too, so let the adventure begin!

With our handbooks in hand (an intended pun), Miss Walls explained what we will be facing in regards to classes and hospital duties. She stated, "You all will be studying at Morgan College for the first semester, then the next two and one half years you will have classes here. Your hospital duties will begin next Saturday and each Saturday thereafter for four hours a day. These duty hours will increase as you progress through the program." Following this announcement, Miss Walls passed out a list of rules, a very long list of rules. If we had seen these prior to applying probably none of us would be here!

Who made these things up? No doubt some sadist who hates young girls. Strict, all encompassing stuff, time schedules, signing in and signing out, a dress code for proper young ladies, no food allowed in our rooms (how could they?) rules for going off campus, times regarding lights out and room checks for neatness, (oh no!). Rules regarding recreation and use of the lounge and TV (one TV for 100+ students), use of the small kitchen and utility room. No phone calls allowed after 10 p.m. on the one and only phone situated in the hallway on each floor, trash pick up, sharing of bathroom facilities, study hall rules, no missing the bus that leaves at 8 a.m. sharp for college 30 miles away, and no missing the bus at 4:30 p.m. to return to hospital grounds. Warnings will be given for rules ignored or broken, with trips to the Nursing Superintendent for serious offenses.

Respect for authority is expected and required by all. Uniforms have not yet arrived but books will be distributed tomorrow afternoon. Please be prompt for all meetings. Next Monday you will be taking the bus to Morgan College and since forty six will be using the five sinks and four toilets, please be up early so everyone can have a turn. Breakfast is at seven a.m. Time yourself accordingly and keep to the schedule with all diligence."

We were asked if we had any questions. No one could speak. She smiled and said "Welcome and good luck, I'm sure you will like it here." I almost burst out laughing, breaking rule #64. Could this be real? Are we ten years old or eighteen? These girls will need bracing up. Some laughter in hidden corners is needed for sure. We were then dismissed with free time to roam about the room and become acquainted with one another.

No one moved. The leaders left the room. Who would be the first to stand? Would a rule be broken? I looked around and someone was getting to her feet. She said "I'm Jo Jo Walker and this will all turn out to be a hoot, believe me! I know someone who went through this whole thing and she is now making ten dollars a day and her whole family thinks she is wonderful. Just hang on and after a few weeks this place will feel just like home." I appreciated the encouragement but what must her home be like?

We all started to mill around and form up in little circles, some chatty and cheerful, others solemn and whispering. I decided what we all needed was a song so I began leading everyone in "Onward Christian Soldiers." By then we were all laughing. Could this place really be so terrible with a group like this? Oh yes, it could. Days ahead would prove it so, but right now we were blissfully ignorant. It was now 8 p.m., lights out at 10 p.m., rule #10, remember? Tomorrow would be a busy day, a tour of Wayside Hospital and further meetings to impart additional information concerning our first weeks here.

Ava and I finally returned to our little hole in the wall. We grabbed up one of our allotted towels (3 a week), our toothbrushes and hurried to stand in line at the bathroom. We have 20 minutes until lights out. It makes one want to push girls away from the sinks. How could that girl named Grace take so long with her teeth? Her hair is already pinned up in neat little rows. How was it possible to look so regal while brushing?

Grateful am I that Dad insisted I pack a flashlight. With "lights out" I can still manage to lay my clothes out for the morning. I can quickly dash the flashlight under a pillow and jump into bed if I hear Miss Stone down the hall. What a day!

Chapter 3
This Alien World
Pauline

We were told to be at breakfast at 8 a.m. Grace, my roommate is already up and moving. It is now 6:45 a.m. I am tired. The first night on the bunk bed was not very comfortable and I had a terrible nightmare. It seems I was locked up in a prison that looked very much like the place I had arrived at yesterday. A wave of melancholy swept over me as I thought about the sad face of my mother when I left. A child of her middle age, I am the last bird to fly away from the nest. All my sisters and brothers are the age of aunts and uncles and I hardly remember when we were all at home together. My home is near the nurses' home and I can go see Mom often. None of my siblings went onto higher education. Hanging on with much determination is my motto; rising above the poverty level is my goal.

After breakfast we reported to our very first class, An Introduction to Nursing. Miss Walls rambled on that for 1½ hours and much of what she talked about I didn't even hear. I was busy looking around at all the girls. A few were classmates of mine in high school. Our school is the largest in the whole county, but I only know two of the six girls who are here. Little did I realize how well I would get to know most of them. First impressions can be so contrary to the true picture.

Touring the Wayside Hospital was next on the agenda. On entering the hospital, its distinct odor overwhelmed me. It smelled something like old adhesive tape and bleach. The 300+ bed facility is shaped like a giant capital T, flanked by stairways. On the first floor is the cafeteria, surrounded by segregated dining rooms (the students are only allowed to dine in their own assigned room). Offices and a pediatric unit are across the top of the T. Two medical-surgical floors take up all the space on the second floor. The surgical unit is on the third floor with another med-surg unit called 3 West. The fourth floor houses the obstetric unit with new mother's rooms, new born nursery, labor rooms and delivery rooms down the spike of the T and another med-surg floor graces the top of the T. The emergency room, pharmacy, x-ray, morgue, Laundry and Housekeeping quarters are all in the dark gloomy basement. There is a newsstand and snack shop on the first floor and an elevator run by a World War II Veteran. He sits on a stool, opens and shuts the doors and directs the elevator up and down the shaft all day long. In the evenings and nights people can push buttons at will. The veteran is quite a captain. I learned later on that it is he who decides who can ride. Doctors and patients are first, nurses and other hospital workers are next and student nurses last. We could very well manage the stairs!

As we walked from place to place there were people everywhere most in a varied collection of uniforms. It was like a sea of ants scurrying here and there all with purpose knowing where to go and what to do. They paid little attention to us, the new "probie" (first year students) class being directed down the hallways and in and out of departments. What a strange, alien place and to think we are destined to become one of the ants and very soon, too!

After dinner that evening, Grace and I sat in our tiny room reviewing it all. What have we done? Well there is no turning back, our nonrefundable fees are paid and we are more or less stuck. It's onward and upward or onward and downward. Only time will tell. "Did you notice how sour faced all the nurses looked? I wonder, will we soon look the same? Also, did you see how they fluttered around the doctors like a bunch of butterflies?" Grace said. The doctors that we saw were not exactly what one would consider handsome. Some are rather ugly in fact. What is the attraction? Do they have unseen attributes? Are they ungodly looking gods? "How about that little short one with his toupee slipping off his head or the one with the flaming red hair and glittering eyes strutting around like he owned the place and looking with distain at everyone and especially us? Let's call the first one 'Slippery' and the second 'Old Red Hood'," she said.

Right then and there we made a pact. Somehow we will manage to keep our spirits up and face it all with as much good humor as we can muster. Laughter always makes the path a little easier and we won't become sour faced either. We will work hard to become angels of mercy not crotchety old witches.

So went our first full day. So much to absorb. Little did we know how familiar everything would become. I would learn much about the beginning and ending of life, more sad moments than happy for the hundreds traveling in and out of the hospital doors. It was place of healing, but often a place where "nothing more can be done." I suppose if all the tears shed could be gathered together there would be a river flowing out the front door and down the hill that Wayside sits on. We never dreamed of what lay ahead. Grace and I would work at Wayside for over forty years.

Chapter 4
No Room to Fail
Reva

After that hurried tour through Wayside even I could see that many improvements were certainly in order and surely the décor needed necessary upgrades. It was unwelcoming and dull. Shouldn't a hospital look bright and cheerful? Little did I realize at the time that any opinions offered by student nurses were promptly ignored. After all we are blank pages on which everyone in that place is eager to write. They will instruct us not the other way around. I suffered through some difficult experiences before that truth took hold. And the crazy rules! Well, rules are made to be broken especially when they make no sense at all. I lived away from home on my own in a large city for several months. Now I must sign in and out! Also the silly regimentation such as no lights after 10 p.m. Is this the middle ages or are we all in some weird convent? Mother Superior (the house mother) was around with her flashlight last night. Jill and I giggled after she left. How could she know who was really in the beds? We need a blackout blind for the window, so we can at least review notes for upcoming tests or maybe write a love letter to some star-struck young fellow. As for personal hygiene, whoever heard of not brushing your teeth after breakfast? Were we to go out of the dining room onto the bus with egg on our teeth? There is a rather dirty looking restroom off the front lobby. Jill and I can sneak in there and brush and at least be able to smile confidently at the boys when we get off the bus at the college. A charming smile is only one of a young girl's assets but an important one.

The first week at Morgan Teachers College was grueling to say the least. Our course load would weary an elephant. Anatomy, physiology, chemistry, microbiology, and all the accompanying labs. We are required to earn a grade of C or above. A grade of D or under and we are tossed out of the nursing program. There are no second chances. We can't return if we fail any of the classes at Morgan. The pressure to pass is constant and the stress level increased dramatically when we met the instructors. On a scale from 0-10 (10 is the best), Mr. Kindle who teaches anatomy and physiology is at most a five. He stalks around the room barking out assignments, stating the tests will be frequent and some will be oral. A skeleton stands in the corner of the classroom on a movable stand and we will be called up front one by one to name all its bones. "Oh Father, our Creator, why did you put so many bones in our hands and feet?" I can visualize many hours of memorizing under the covers with a flashlight or a dimly lit lamp with the blackout blind down. Bones will be easy compared to muscles and nerves in addition to their origins and insertions.   Thankfully the skeleton doesn't have those muscles and nerves attached. Those tests will be written.

Chemistry and microbiology, that teacher is terrible, a zero on the scale for sure. He simply doesn't teach anything and gives no explanations regarding the contents of his tests. He just says, "Read your books. Tomorrow we will test on chapters five through twelve." You must be kidding! Thank goodness I had chemistry in high school, so I can at least understand what is going on. Poor Jill doesn't have a clue about chemistry and we are instructed on how to look into the microscope with both eyes open and Jill just can't get the hang of it. How can she identify parts of cells or bacteria if she can't see them? Much prayer is needed on her behalf.

They divided our class into two groups. My group stopped at "J" and Jill is an "L", so I'm not even in class with her. She cries a lot. I try to cheer her up and she seems to brighten up after a joke or two. Laughter truly is the best medicine and I give her spoonsful at every opportunity. I make up stories about Mother Superior's probably very racy private life. No doubt she sneaks out after bed check to meet some old fellow and they do things good girls should never talk about. We both howl. Troubles are forgotten for a while and we savor our time alone here in our tiny niche, our escape place.

Chapter 5
The Devil is in the Details
Rachael

Our first four days at Morgan College are at last over (one week). My head feels at least two sizes larger because so much information has been dumped into it. Now I have to separate and categorize, so it will be in some recognizable order. Today is Friday and we have classes at the nurses' home all day long. These classes are to prepare us for "hands on nursing." My dream since fifth grade was to become a registered nurse. Taking care of the sick seems like such a high calling. I like people and with nursing I will be personally involved with the folks. I wonder what chemistry class has to do with that, plus all those other facts that are parading through my head? It must all be necessary. After all, the "powers that be" have included all this seemingly unrelated stuff in our course work.

At least I know the instructor who is teaching "Principles of Nursing." We live on the very same street in town. A nurse in England during World War II, she met her GI soldier, married him and they came to America. He has a dental practice in the city. Mrs. Simmons lives just three houses down in a lovely white stucco house surrounded by her very own English Country garden. My father died when I was seven and my mother turned our home in to a boarding house to make ends meet. She kept a garden out back and she and Mrs. Simmons would talk often about how to grow potatoes, tomatoes and such. They also both love flowers of all kinds. The dry English wit of Mrs. Simmons kept us laughing and I loved hearing her accent. I'm hoping she doesn't act like she knows me here. I have had some very bad experiences with the teacher's pet thing.

On Saturday we will spend four hours on duty at Wayside with our first real live patient. I know how to do nothing; hopefully Mrs. Simmons will have us a little prepared.

We have not yet received our uniforms so we were told to wear when on duty - a sensible blouse, skirt, white hose and our nurses' shoes. Arriving at the hospital in such attire will be awkward indeed. What will the poor patient think? A student nurse who has not even been issued a uniform yet! How bizarre is that? I am sure he or she will feel they are receiving proper care.

Mrs. Simmons introduced herself and didn't seem to notice me (Relief). Then she began instructing on how to make a bed properly, how to make a bed with a person in it, how to wind the bed up and down, how to position the bed side table for meals, how to assist with meal trays, and how to turn a patient. There is a hospital bed in the classroom with an adult sized dummy lying in it. Her name is Mrs. Chase. She (Mrs. Simmons, not Mrs. Chase) demonstrated how to place a bedpan under the dummy and how to remove it without spilling the contents. The bed pan is then covered with a small towel, taken to the utility room, placed in a thing called a hopper and flushed. Then Mrs. Simmons added, "Don't just toss the bedpan in the hopper with wild abandon it might spill about. If there is stool and urine in the bedpan, urine amount can be estimated (what a relief). The stool deposits must be noted and described – liquid, soft, hard, color (very important) how much, small, medium or large amount and this information is to be accurately recorded in the patient's chart in the proper place. All urine must be measured before disposal. The urine amount (including color and odor) must also be charted. The urine amounts are added up every eight hours and then the final total in 24 hours." This information is apparently very important. Unbelievable! A thirty five minute lecture combined with accompanying demonstrations about dealing with nasty body functions doesn't exactly fit my lofty dreams of becoming a professional nurse. However for sure, I will be getting very personal with the folks. Much of this, I am thinking, is going to be extremely unpleasant and this is only the emptying of bed pans and urinals, not wiping and cleaning patients' bottoms also included in today's instructions. I was to learn later bedpan duty was never ever over. I would empty hundreds. Other nasty things were ahead, bed pan duty would pale in comparison.

Mrs. Simmons is very funny and we were amused by her English humor and accent, our first nice teacher. She told us we will have others to help us on the floor (nursing units are called "being on the floor"). Is this a pun? There will be nurses' aides and orderlies to assist us and we will always have Nursing instructors to teach us, two on each Medical Surgical Unit and also in all the specialties. My mind is a little relieved, but I still feel rather anxious. How will it all turn out? Time marches on and tomorrow is getting closer by the minute. Oh dear!

Chapter 6
The Nitty Gritty
Katie

Saturday morning, 6:30 a.m. We are all having breakfast and we are to report on duty to our assigned floor for the very first time at 7 a.m. I can hardly eat. My stomach is moving around dramatically and shooting small bullets of nausea up into my throat. What will my first patient be like? Will she like me? Her name is Constance Miller and her room number is 244. She expects to benefit from an experienced nurse. Instead she will have inexperienced me for two and one half hours! I think I can place a bedpan properly and assist with minor needs, but all else in regards to nursing is a big fat unknown. We haven't had the final go ahead for changing the bed with a patient in it and neither have we learned how to give a bed bath. We are also without uniforms. Mrs. Miller will think I walked in off the street. Only my name tag gives away my real reason for being here, Katie Hatter, student nurse. It should read "Katie Hatter, weak kneed coward." Well, Mama always told me getting started was always hardest. She died when I was only nine and was sick for months before, in and out of the hospital many times. She told me she loved most of the nurses. The good ones always knew what she needed even before she asked and they could make her comfortable in the bed when she was so sick and couldn't tolerate getting up. Mrs. Summers told us this was called "anticipating the patient's needs." Apparently this is a very big deal and if a nurse can't do this one big thing well, she is of little account. Well, here I am. I have no idea what Mrs. Miller will need if she doesn't tell me. I am a failure before even starting out.

Six of us go to Two North and will have two nursing instructors, teaching and supervising, a Miss Kirby and a Mrs. House. First we all stood around listening to a detailed report about all the patients on the unit during the last shift, also what horrors were planned for them this day. Some are to be cut up (surgery), others will go through mysterious procedures, x-rays, catherizations, wound dressings, enemas, labs, etc., etc. I listened carefully for Mrs. Constance Miller; nothing is apparently planned for this a.m. She does however require assistance with eating and with all personal care. It seems she has suffered a CVA, whatever that is.

After the report, Miss Kirby took me to Mrs. Miller's room and introduced us. Mrs. Miller looked very much put out. She said "Who am I, some guinea pig? These hospitals just like to practice on people." Miss Kirby reassured her, "Now Mrs. Miller, Miss Hatter is here to help you. All of us started out like this young lady. Try to be a patient patient." Then Miss Kirby left!

Mrs. Miller looked at me with great suspicion, but then a gleam came to her eye. Here is a slave of her very own. She knew all about the slave part, a mother of six and probably married to a very demanding husband. This is now her chance to be on the other end of things. At least that must have been her thoughts because the whole time I was there she barked commands. "Lift my leg, the right one, not the left. A drink of water, I need a drink of water. My teeth haven't been brushed for two days. No one ever helps me with my meals and here comes breakfast. My hands need to be washed. I need the bed pan before I eat. You don't have me sitting right on that bed pan. My tail end hurts. Be careful, don't spill it in the bed. Sometimes it takes hours to be get a clean sheet around here. My coffee isn't hot and would you look at that egg? The cook must be off sick today." On and on she went, "anticipating needs" was not needed here. I was dancing to her tune for sure, a fast fox trot. I did my best and tried to be patient with my patient. Heavens above, did I really feel like slapping her? Where was that compassionate and understanding nurse I dreamed I would be regardless of the situation? She apparently left the room sometime after the first one half hour, leaving an irritated and annoyed me behind. I couldn't wait to get out and follow her.   Finally 10:30 a.m. came, time to escape. I told dear complaining Mrs. Miller goodbye (and good riddance).   What had just happened to me, little Miss Florence Nightingale, persistent in the face of persecution? This needs a whole new looking into. My hope for the next time is someone else a little more pleasant and maybe, just maybe, the experience will be a little more encouraging. If not I am in real trouble. I could actually hate nursing and I am stuck with it. After all, there are appearances to be kept up and families not to disappoint.

It seems that most of the other girls fared much better than I. Are they telling the truth? I didn't join in the conversation. I couldn't bear to talk about the disaster in Room 244 with patient Constance Miller.

During the days ahead I discovered there are plenty of Mrs. Millers and other girls didn't hesitate talking about their bad experiences quite openly to other students. Complaining has become very common place, the norm, so to speak. After a few months no one would admit to actually liking anything. Misery really does love company. In fact misery could be our middle names. How does that sound, Kathy "Misery" Hatter? Perfect!

Chapter 7
Hurry Up! The Bus is Here!
Grace

We are rushing ahead to board that stupid old bus. It is waiting outside the front entrance of the hospital with its motor running. After the first week everyone has picked out all their seats. You would think that they had their names on them. Yesterday I almost sat down in Mabel Eisel's seat. Heaven forbid! She looked daggers at me so I moved on. It was tempting to just tell her off, but I thought better of it. "Grin and bear it Grace", I said to myself. "You may need Mabel as a friend someday." The letters "C" and "E" are close together and I am getting to know the girls through alphabetic closeness. Someone told me Mabel came from another county west of ours, the one with lots of farms. Her clothes speak of long and tender care, a bit shabby but can handle lots of washing and hanging on lines. I'm a city girl myself and I love the shops downtown with all those lovely outfits displayed in the windows. Mother managed to buy a few really nice things for me to wear here. Some will require expensive dry cleaning, so great care is needed. I'm sure to stay away from Mabel. She throws up almost every morning on the way to breakfast. "Homesick", her roommate tells everyone.

What a ride, books on our laps, sliding as we go around turns! The bus driver is quite unfriendly. He looks at us getting on and off with great indifference. Can't wait to have a coffee, I guess.

I'm worried about my bobby socks, are they evenly folded and in place? There is so little time to get ready but I'm getting more efficient. Looking around I see I am managing better than most. What a rag tag group we are, except for a few. Most consider matching and color coordination down at the bottom of the list. No wonder uniforms are considered necessary. An improvement for most, that's for sure. So much for dress, I need to be reciting names of muscles in my head and thinking about where they are located and how they work together to promote movement. Two tests this morning, one in anatomy and one in physiology. Mr. Kindle has no mercy.

Mornings on the bus there is very little chattering. Most look dazed and worried. However on the way back everyone tries to talk at once. I almost always get a headache, so the quiet this morning is nice. I do believe the girls in the front rows are after Feona again. There she goes to lead us in some silly songs. It does lighten the ride. She is quite good, the singing speeds up and slows down according to her direction. Loud and soft is managed by lowering or raising her arms and she has this

16

very loud infectious laugh. It makes me want to laugh too. Laughter really is contagious. There has to be something special about someone who is able to lift the mood of this crowd. "You are My Sunshine", well, there is little reality in that. What a gray day, fog all about and misty, cold rain. So much for the polished shoes. I will be glad when these daily commutes are over.

Breakfast had to be eaten so fast that I'm hungry already for lunch. The food is terrible at the college. Even their hot dogs taste awful. How can a hot dog be ruined? We eat everything regardless. It will be a while till dinner and hunger stalks us. Dinner at the hospital will be much better. The food is good even though we have to gulp it down. Arriving back from Morgan at 5 p.m., we must be in our places for study hall at 6 p.m., sit there until 8 p.m. and the librarian, Mrs. Watters, will be walking around monitoring us lest we actually speak or make the slightest noise. Why is it every evening I feel like screaming? We are like intimidated sheep, silent and obedient, reading, turning pages and taking notes. Looking over at Pauline we both groan. Will 8 p.m. ever come so we can get out of here and let loose a little? We will have two whole hours before Mrs. Stone blinks the hall lights and then turns them off and begins her flashlight ritual. Hopefully, I will have time to put my hair up, brush my teeth, polish my shoes and lay out tomorrow's coordinated outfit.

I need to be up very early tomorrow morning – first in the shower, only one is in working order. This morning, Reva Flanagan was in there splashing and singing. I'll set the alarm 15 minutes earlier and maybe I'll beat her to it.

This schedule we are on is a killer. It feels like I'm on a tread mill running, not walking. Saturday afternoon can't arrive soon enough. Can it really only be Tuesday?

Chapter 8
Dressed for the Job
Jo Jo

I have been here in nursing school for three weeks and just today we were given our uniforms. I am so thrilled! I can hardly remember when I didn't want to be a nurse, at least since the second grade. There was a nurse living down the road from my house and I used to see her waiting for her ride to the hospital dressed in a beautiful white uniform, envy, envy you are a curse. Well this is at least a start. They might not yet be all white, but we were handed out three blue and white stripped uniforms with white collars and cuffs with "Miss Walker" embroidered on the left cuff, three all white aprons with studs to hold the apron on. They hook at the back waistline. Also included is a blue sweater and a pair of bandage scissors. The older students put the scissors at the back between those studs so when needed they just pull them out. Very neat! I tried it all on and I was transformed. I look so nursy (Is that a word?). Maybe my dream can actually become true!

I keep thinking about all I had to do just to get in this school. High school grades had to be at least a "C" or higher, application forms needed to be filled out. I had to endure a physical and dental exam, shots, entrance tests and then that nerve wracking interview with the Superintendent of Nurses, Mrs. Rivers. We had to have a parent with us so Mom and I went on the bus. I couldn't sleep the night before worrying about how I would hold up during the dreaded meeting.

Arriving at the hospital, we were told to sit in the outer office and Mrs. Rivers would see us soon. I wanted to bite my nails, but held off. After waiting there for ten very long minutes, we were called in.

There sits Mrs. Rivers behind her desk, very stern looking. Her auburn hair streaked with gray was pulled back into a severe bun. Her blouse was ruffled at the neck and she had lots of jangly jewelry on, her glasses were hanging around her neck on one of those old woman elastic things. She reminded me of a portrait I saw not long ago of Queen Elizabeth I, regal but ugly. She looked at me with watery faded blue eyes and I am sure she is at least fifty. Why is she still working at her age?

"So, Josephine", she said "I understand from reading your application that you really want to be a nurse so you can help the sick. Have you ever been around anyone who was ill?" "Yes Mame", I answered in a shaky voice. "My Aunt Eleanor was once sick for five weeks and I helped her whenever I could, I also volunteered at school in the nurses' room, and I help take care of my Aunt Mary's baby – who is sick a lot."

The 'old queen' didn't look a bit impressed. She just looked bored. Boy, this wasn't going well. Five minutes had gone by and it seemed like at least a week. Would my deodorant hold out? My underarms were dripping. Did they have the room this hot on purpose? Finally after many more stupid questions, "Do I do well away from home? Do I participate in physical fitness activities? Do I get along well with my peers and those in authority over me?" Yes, yes and more yeses. Who in their right mind would say no?

Finally she stood up and said, "Josephine, you will hear from this office by next Tuesday. Your grades are just good enough, so you will need to work very hard and keep on course if accepted."

So here I am wavering off course, especially with that ridiculous chemistry class. One of my friends who is attending Morgan college had Mr. Steward for another course and she said he pays little attention to grades. He just fails those students he doesn't like. So stay under the radar. If he doesn't know you he can't like or dislike you. For once in my life a "W" appears to be a lucky letter. I'm sitting at the back of the class hiding behind a 'T'. If I can make it over this giant hurdle it will be a miracle for sure. I really want to wear a nurse's uniform so I'm forging ahead with great determination and lots of "Hail Mary's".

On Saturday we will wear our uniforms for the first time, on duty! I must make sure everything is in order. My hair clean and neat and off the collar, no heavy makeup, nails clean and cut with no polish, shoes polished with no scuff marks, white hose with no runners (note – clear nail polish will stop a runner in it's tracks). No perfume! Some patients may be allergic. No offensive body odor emanating from students will be tolerated. Bad odors from patients must be okay. I've smelled some really bad ones already.

The hospital laundry will wash up our uniforms weekly. Soiled ones must be put in the hall hamper at the nurses' home each Thursday and picked up at the laundry the following Tuesday. No dirty aprons allowed on duty. We have been issued enough so each student can look clean and neat. A visit to Mrs. Rivers will be required if a student's appearance is not acceptable. I'll beg, borrow or steal one of my roommate's aprons before I'll risk another encounter with her Highness, Queen Elizabeth. She must be avoided at all costs.

Oh, I must hurry, our class with Mrs. Summers begins in five minutes. Today we are to finish learning how to bathe a patient in bed and tomorrow we have to actually do that to a <u>real</u> person. Another hurdle ahead! Just thirty five more months to go once this week is over. I feel like the "Little Engine that Could", puffing along for miles with the end of the line nowhere in sight.

Chapter 9
What's that in my Mashed Potatoes?
Feona

The classes at Morgan are overwhelming, starting at 9 a.m. until 4 p.m. We go from one class or lab to another all day long. One day a week we have a half day off. On Thursday afternoons some of us go over to the girl's dorm lounge, sit down, put our feet up and watch the television. My favorite show is "Queen for a Day." There are four ladies who tell their sad, sappy stories and after each tale the audience claps and shouts and this registers on some kind of voice machine. The lady who receives the loudest applause is crowned "Queen for a Day." Lots of wonderful prizes are given to her and her family, vacations, cars, jewelry, cash, etc., etc. We express our opinions by clapping and shouting and adding our input over who should win and we hoot and holler if our pick is crowned. The show is a great diversion and a nice break from the relentless schedule we are enduring.

I would like to kiss the person or persons who invented television. I love it. My Mom and Dad think that people who own TV sets have money to throw away and that it is a luxury only to be considered if your bills are all paid and there is cash for the purchase. Folks who buy such luxury items on time are very irresponsible. However, my parents trot over to my Aunt Betty's house every Saturday evening to watch The Perry Como Show and she doesn't have money pouring out her ears. Once I have a job, I am going to buy a TV even if I have to eat oatmeal for breakfast every day for years and I hate oatmeal.

Am I really going through all this crazy nursing school business for a TV? Why am I here anyhow? I guess I can blame my older sister. She wanted to be a nurse and my parents were so pleased and happy. She went through all the necessary preparations and then met the love of her life and instead got married (the marriage is apparently now on the rocks) and never went into training. Mom and Dad grieved over all this. They were so disappointed. Becoming a nurse to them is like becoming First Lady, a golden opportunity to really move up in life. So I decided that I would go in for them. Pleasing Mom and Dad would be payback for all they have given up for me over the years. If I can just finish and become a honest to goodness nurse, I will make Mom 'Queen for Day' for sure on Graduation Day.

One day we were in the dreaded anatomy class with the full sized skeleton. Located up front hanging on a moving rack. I noticed a skull, creepy really, sitting on a nearby table. That day we were discussing teeth, of all things, and I looked at that skull. The teeth were all loose and covered with tarter. I whispered to Susie who was sitting in front of me, "Look at that disgusting thing. It must be at least one hundred years old." Susie agreed and stuttered. "For sure dental hygiene wasn't at the top of his list." What made me do it? I don't know. When no one was looking, I took one of the loose teeth and put it in my pocket, a grand souvenir.

That evening I was off the bus first and first in line for dinner. I love this because those first served have more time to eat and the food was especially good that evening, roast beef with mashed potatoes and gravy, green beans and rolls with butter. My friend, Susie, was sitting across the table from me and again I can't explain why, but when she turned her head, I stuck that tooth right down into her mashed potatoes. Fork to mouth, I watched her and she put the tooth into her mouth. Wow! She spit it out and let out an ear piercing scream. She stood up and looked straight at me and shouted "Feona, this time you have gone too far! It's a tooth from that awful skull, isn't it? Why would you put that dirty revolting thing in my food?"

Everyone look shocked and appalled and I felt truly awful. What is wrong with me? Dead silence, then everyone began to laugh and believe it or not, Susie started to laugh too. What a relief! I wouldn't be tarred and feathered after all!

The next day in anatomy class that skull was a major item of interest. It sat there grinning at us with one missing tooth. I think he somehow knew how badly we all needed comic relief.

Chapter 10
Goodbye and Good Riddance
Lindsay

At last, at last the day is here! We will not be returning ever again to Morgan College. September until the middle of January we have made that bus trip four days a week, days full of seemingly unending classes, studying and tests. We were given only two weeks off during the Christmas holidays. One of those weeks we were on hospital duty and the other we were allowed to go home. The week at home was borrowed from our month off in the summer.

Home for Christmas and what a lovely time it was. All my immediate and extended family were together for Christmas dinner. We were at Grandma's house for most of the day. To top it all off, there was a beautiful snowfall that morning, a truly lovely white Christmas. We went sledding and made a huge snowman. It was wonderful to be away from Wayside. I didn't want to go back. Final exams loomed ahead at Morgan.

Now the finals are over. Did I pass? I don't feel a bit encouraged. The tests were so difficult. It's possible I could be going home for good. We were told that usually up to ten students each year are unable to make the required grades and have to leave.

Now we are all lined up to get on the bus for the last time. Was that a collective sigh of relief I heard? The first great hurdle is now behind us. If we survive we will be moving forward in this strange adventure. The unknown future is viewed with anxiety for sure by everyone.

When very small I lived in town, but after first grade I went to live with my Grandma. Dad was away in the army and Mother was working at a dress shop downtown. Everyone thought my brother and I would be better watched over with lots of family around and I love the country. The bus ride to school was long, down country roads through woods and fields. Each season is unique. I love the fall best, so colorful. Now I am back where I started – in town, so bleak in winter.

My decision to go into nursing was mostly because Mother said that a nurse would always have a job and wouldn't be laid off like she had been four times. So off I went to Wayside, a country girl now living in the fast lane, quickly learning about a completely different way of life. Farms and fields are only seen on weekends.

Looking back I will have to say there were challenges but also some advantages to going off together to the college on that bus. Boys were there! College girls apparently resented the influx of added competition. They weren't at all friendly. Being with fellow nursing students caused us to

22

hang together and learn about each other. After all, we were all dealing with the same crazy schedule and impossible classes. Connected, we are becoming. We came from so many different places and varied situations all thrown together in one boat or should I say, bus?

Before coming to Wayside, I already knew a few of the girls. My roommate, Agnes, is one of my best friends and I remember Feona. We were both cheerleaders and when our high schools met for basketball games I would see her. Before the games all of the cheerleaders huddled together and talked. Then each squad would to go their side of the gym. The cheers would be loud and the pompoms would dance. It wasn't just the basketball players that were competing. Who could forget Feona? She was a laugh a minute. Now here we are student nurses and since we are both "H's". We sit next to each other in most classes, the extrovert with the introvert. She often says things and does things I wish I had the nerve to do.

Everyone tells me Pauline Macey and I look a lot alike. We both have dark hair and are about the same weight and height. Sometimes people at the hospital get us mixed up. Pauline and I were becoming best friends.

We will now have all our classes at the nurse's home, five days a week. We will be on duty every weekday morning, a break for lunch, then classes all afternoon. No more evening study halls! We no longer work a half day on Saturdays, so Friday evenings we can go home. Just the thought of getting away gives me a reason to endure another week.

So goodbye to the bus, hooray, and a final goodbye to Morgan. You won't be missed. Things may be beginning to look up!

Chapter 11
The Grades are Here!
Jill

Told to go down to the large classroom, we filed in and took our seats, in alphabetical order, of course. The grades from Morgan College have arrived and today we will discover the bitter truth. Everyone looks rather grim. How will we face our families if we fail and are "kicked out?" "Kicked out" is the phrase everyone uses. One is not dismissed or sent off with honor, but "kicked out" in disgrace. I could already hear the comments from relatives. "Well, of course we all know Jill, poor thing, isn't very smart. It takes brains to become a nurse. She probably didn't try hard enough. She tends to be a little lazy, don't you think? You know how these young people are these days. They want everything handed to them on a silver platter. Why in my day, we knew what hard work was. If only we had the opportunities girls have today. 'Kicked out'. Well, who among us is surprised?"

Miss Walls walked into the room and looked around to make sure all forty six of us were present and accounted for. She explained, "Each one of you will be called into my office individually, one at a time. If you did not pass, your family will be notified by phone immediately after you are told. Then you will go and pack your things and leave today, if possible. You must be off the premises by tomorrow at the latest. Now, Miss Arnold, will you follow me out please?"

Whew, how brutal was that? Of course in my mind I was already pulling out Grandma's old suitcase and throwing in my clothes. I must not let anyone know how devastating this failure will be. Can I keep a stiff upper lip when my lower one is trembling? Well, I suppose it will be back to the five and ten cent store. I never passed one chemistry test, only my Chemistry labs were "C's" and above and that was because my partner was Rachel. I was in a fog the whole time. The only thing I know for sure is H_2O is water. Right now I need a drink.

A, B, C, D, E, F, all the girls came back in the room and sat down – passed! "G" went out and came back. She announced, "Hey everyone, I'm going home. Hated it here anyhow. This is a happy day!" "H, I, J" all sat down, relief evident on their faces. "L." That was me! Feeling like a failure and shaking like a leaf, I sat down in front of Miss Wall's desk. Knees really can knock! She looked at me, frowning. I think, since I have been here I can remember her smiling, once. "Well, Miss Lee," she said, "it seems that you have passed. Anatomy – B, Physiology – C,

Microbiology –B and Chemistry – B." WHAT? Surely she is mistaken. She must have read off Rachel Lucas' grades instead. But no, it was true. The chemistry professor gave me a "B." There really is a God who rewards the undeserving. Right now if Mr. Stewart were here, I would kiss his wrinkled cheek. I can go back and sit with those other brilliant girls, if only I'm able to stand up and walk.

Somehow I made myself move out the door and headed for the room. Is there a cure for a nervous breakdown? I sat down, rather in a state of shock. I wouldn't be going home in disgrace after all, at least not today.

On and on the torture continued until we were down to the "W's." At the end of the afternoon thirty eight passed, a loss of seven. One girl left before today. She had fallen madly in love with a guy at Morgan and is getting married in a few weeks. Why couldn't that have happened to me?

Such a brutal day, called for some sort of celebration for those left standing. Though our hearts were heavy for the girls who had to leave, some exited in bitter tears, we couldn't entirely mask our relief.

Reva and I skipped and laughed up the stairs. There was much shouting when we reached the third floor. One of the more limber among us did a few cartwheels down the hall. The smokers, smoked, the most relieved collapsed in their bunks and those who lost their roommates wiped away tears. The phone was busy all evening. For thirty-eight of us our families' honor was preserved and we were alive to fight another day.

I went for two cokes and Reva and I drank a solemn toast and threw dead tree twigs out our window (they had been part of our décor). Then we joined some others for a few hours of laughter and song.

When Mrs. Stone came around for room check that night we feigned sleep, but we were both wide awake, sleep was elusive. Who could sleep after such a day?

Chapter 12
The Post
Pauline

I understand that everybody dies and surely this is one of life's greatest mysteries, but to a girl of eighteen, it seemed like something that only happened to others. I don't remember my dad at all. I was only three when he died. So it was just my mother and me at home. My brothers and sisters are all married and had their own families. So seeing someone I know dead seems way out there. Of course I realize that becoming a nurse I will be dealing with life and death, but in February of that first year such things were far from my thoughts. So I became a little anxious and nervous when I heard that as first year students we are required to attend a post. A post, what was that? Well, actually, it is an autopsy performed to discover the cause of death, a post mortem. Woe! Wait a minute! I wasn't ready for that. Hopefully the call would never come.

That fated evening, we were finished with dinner and all back at the nurses' home and the phone rang. Ginger answered it and shouted down the hallway, "We are to report to the morgue at 6:30 sharp. The doctor will be there to do a post! Miss Walls will check our names off a list as we arrive. Everyone is required to attend."

With anxiety mounting and my stomach rumbling, I joined all the others and off we went down into the dark, dreary basement and into the awful gloomy room. What was that strange smell? "Formaldehyde", someone whispered, "a chemical that is used to preserve dead things." Ugh! How creepy our surroundings, jars of body parts sat around the room on shelves. The place was quite dark except for a large bright light focused on a big table centered in the middle of the room where a body of a large old man lay. A white sheet covered his legs and abdomen. His color was stone gray. He definitely looked dead. This was far and away from being fun, a Halloween scene that was real. Even the doctor looked morbid standing there in his white scrubs with his dark hair sticking out around a white surgical cap and a sober look on his face.

I stood around the outer edge as we crowded into the room, my dinner still moving around in my stomach. Do we really have to see this person cut up? If only I could sit down somewhere and close my eyes but there are no chairs in a morgue. No one wants to linger here.

After a few words of welcome and introduction, the doctor picked up a scalpel (a small surgical knife) and started to cut that poor dead man right down the middle of his chest. The room was deadly silent, no one moved Just then I heard some shuffling and a thud. Oh my, was that Jill?

She just hit the floor in a dead faint (bad word choice). Then I heard another thud, there went Susie with a follow-up! Everyone was moving about and trying to help the two victims. Two girls carried Jill into the hallway followed by two carrying Susie and both were helped into wheelchairs, listless and pale. They were rushed off to the emergency area just down the hall.

That brought the whole disturbing event to a screeching halt and we were dismissed and all trotted back to our rooms. After that incident "the mandatory Post" would no longer be part of the student nurses' training program. We were saved by our two heroes who did what most of us felt like doing and probably would have joined in had the dissecting continued.

I did hear later on that our class is the only one with fainting members in recent memory. What a bunch of wimps we are. Miss Walls told us that our faces looked like we had just exited the theater after a horror movie. She began to lecture us. "Really, you all must get it together, this is medicine after all. You must learn how to handle your emotions. Nurses are not emotional, but stoic. You need to bear up and absorb shocking things without your faces expressing your feelings and for goodness sakes, fainting is unacceptable. Nurses don't faint! Don't we realize patients will be looking at us for support and comfort? If we fall apart in uncomfortable circumstances, things will quickly become chaotic. We are to help not hinder."

So hiding our feelings inside our starched uniforms is a lesson we all need to learn. We must learn to act as mature stable persons. Not revealing any inner turmoil. I suppose we must find other ways to express our pent up emotions. We began to turn recreational activities and free time into avenues of escape. Some of the things we came up with for stress relief bordered on the extreme, but that's a story for another day. Somehow I know I will never forget this one.

Chapter 13
You Mean, You Didn't Learn That?
Jo Jo

From now on all our classes and "hands-on" nursing instruction will be at the hospital or nurses' home, except for a three month stint at one of the state mental hospitals during our last year. From the very beginning of this stage we are kept insanely busy. The basic teaching at Morgan just laid the ground work for what will be taught here. We will all attend classes together, all thirty-eight of us. Mrs. Caskey will be our instructor for Medical-Surgical Nursing.

On the first day, after four hours of exhausting hospital duty with constant nagging from our nursing instructors, we met for class and Mrs. Caskey sailed into the room five minutes late. I say sailed because she looked like an eagle that landed among us. She had a bird-like face, a large beak of a nose, and dark, piercing, glittering eyes. Her graying hair was pulled back in a knot at her neck and her nurse's cap sat on her head, kind of looked like a pot. By now we knew that every nursing school has its own distinctive cap. Some literally look like nurses caps but others might look like most anything from a piece of lace on the head to one with pleats and tucks, all shapes and sizes. Wayside caps are very traditional looking.

Our Nursing Handbook had Mrs. Caskey listed as a RN with a BS degree after her name. She apparently graduated from a nursing school in Vermont and a college in Kentucky. How she ended up here is anybody's guess.

She looked at us with an air of disdain as if she couldn't imagine any way she could whip us up into worthwhile nurses but was determined to give it her best shot.

She first outlined the course (160 credit hours). "You had the foundation prepared at the college and now we will be examining all the body systems individually to discover all that may go wrong and what the medical community is prepared to do in the way of treatment, prevention and correction. Today we will begin with the digestive system, page 82 in your textbooks. First we will review a little of the anatomy and physiology to get our minds on the right track."

Oh boy, Mr. Kindle at Morgan College never got to the digestive system. He spent so much time on the circulatory system after bones, muscles and nerves, that we only advanced through one-half both anatomy and physiology books. I can still hear him saying, "the heart has one beat that sounds like lub dub, lub dub, lub dub." He seemed fascinated with the blood pouring in and out of that incredible organ and I must agree it all is very amazing.

Anyhow, here we are sitting, dumb as posts. She began to ask questions, "What is connected to the stomach, and what comes next, what is the difference between the small and large intestines and so on?" We all had blank looks on our faces. The system that begins at the mouth and ends at an unmentionable place has a number of mysterious parts and connections, a long internal tube that we know little or nothing about.

After not being able to answer any of her questions, she began to realize that the foundation we should have we didn't. She would need to begin with anatomy and physiology, like doing double duty. She ranted on about that for a while, as if it was our fault Mr. Kindle got stuck on the heart. So off we go onto another fast track to learning, double trouble and double studying.

I could feel myself gearing up for another huge hurtle. Was there any other job where one could wear a white uniform? "Once started, one must finish", another of my mother's frequent quotes.

Our assignment was to come to class the next day able to name all the parts of the digestive system and what each did in regards to the digestion of food. Really? Then and only then will she be able to teach us about how it all could go wrong. That was not our only class either, Drugs and Solutions follows immediately afterward. Miss Walls is our instructor and she is constantly going on about the metric system, whatever that is.

All of this sinks my plans for this evening. I was dreaming of going down to the lounge, Coke in hand to watch Wagon Train. Such is life. In this place no plan is safe. I am learning how to adjust. Each day brings its own surprises and disappointments. One hundred and sixty hours with "a face like an eagle", who could bear it? There is some comfort in knowing that none of us will be watching Wagon Train tonight.

Chapter 14
The Prettiest Cell on the Block
Reva

Rumor has been going around for weeks and it is now a known fact. An addition to the nurses' residence is to begin next week. The goal is to have it finished so our class can move over there in September when next year's "probie" class arrives. The stair wells at the end of the right side of our building will be removed, right at the end of our hallway. We had been given notice as to how to go over to the hospital without going near the new construction area. The plan includes two floors of rooms for students and the bottom floor will house a new library, additional classrooms and offices. The lodging rooms will be twice as large as our rooms now with two beds (no more bunk beds) two bedside stands, two chairs and two desks, plus two dressers with a large mirror. Also, each room will have two large closets. Just think, one for each of us. We all need to hang on in this place just for a chance to live in the new non-cramped space. Excitement abounds!

Our present room looks much nicer than the day Jill and I took occupancy. Mama gave us two rugs she made last winter. She cuts up old clothing into strips, sews them together in one long continuous string and rolls these into balls. She then plats the rolls and when finished, sews the plats into large circles or oblong rugs. The ones she gave us are bright red with blue and green. I discovered in an old trunk upstairs two nice bed spreads and added these to our décor.

But first, I decided the room needed a complete and thorough cleaning. So Jill and I gathered some cleaning supplies from the janitor's room and began by moving the bunk bed around the room. Jill could reach the ceiling and upper walls. Because of my fear of heights, I tackled scrubbing the lower walls. This necessary cleaning must have been ignored for years! The dirty green walls turned out to be a lighter, brighter color and we had to throw many buckets of dirty water off the porch balcony. Next the very dirty window! After much coaxing, Jill agreed to hang out the window if I would hold on to her. I gave her a wet soapy cloth and she leaned outside, her feet on the sill fifty feet up. I held her legs and she scrubbed away years of dirt and grime. What a difference! It was worth every scary moment. We could see across the way and down the hill and the added light allowed in was a great improvement. I told Jill it was worth talking her out of her protests. Though very pale, she agreed.

So a clean room, new rugs, bed coverings, and a few pictures for the walls, plus a calendar and our room is transformed! Also for a fresh touch, grabbed a few flowering mums from one of the yards down the street. They are now sitting in a milk bottle on the dresser. Very nice.

Some of the other rooms you wouldn't even want to walk into, especially those that have four girls, clothes everywhere, books and papers lying about, ash trays filled with cigarette butts, and unmade beds. Believe me, there is some hurrying and scurrying about when the day comes for room checks. Demerits are given for messy rooms and if one receives thirty demerits one is "campused". That means no leaving the grounds for a stated time mostly two, but maybe up to six weeks. Demerits can also be acquired for other rule infractions. Too many can lead to suspension and being "kicked out." A sure way for immediate dismissal is to marry. During the last six months one may marry with permission but not before. We know of one girl, Amy, who is married and keeping it, of course, secret. It's like a dance in the dark for Amy, trying to keep anyone higher up from finding out. Some leaks apparently did reach Mrs. Rivers. She called Amy in with her mother and demanded to be told the truth. Both denied that she was married. What a mother! She could lie to Mrs. Rivers! My mama would tell the truth and I would be working in some business office somewhere, my nursing career in shambles with "you made your bed now lie in it" ringing in my ears. All previous blood, sweat and tears, wasted.

Oh well, tomorrow I will have three patients to give "a.m". care before 11 a.m. Last week we had two. Whoever is in charge of this race certainly doesn't have to run it. At least I can collapse at the end of the day in the prettiest cell on the block.

Chapter 15
The English Gentleman Teaches English
Feona

A notice on the board from the educational director today informed us since we didn't have the required English course at Morgan, an English professor will be sent here. The class will be held every Thursday at 1:00 pm for six weeks.

We were all sitting in our seats waiting for Mr. Hunter on that first Thursday. Looking out the small basement window we watched as he came up the walk. He walked through the door and we observed a very large man with a large round face, sweating and puffing from the exertion of walking up hill. After walking into the room, he looked at us sitting on our chairs and his face became very red. He opened his mouth and began to stutter and spit out a few words introducing himself, "Ump, I'm Mr. Hunter here to teach you a required English course. I assume you are already in possession of the textbook we will be using. I am positive all you bright young ladies will do well. There will be a few small quizzes and a paper to write after you have learned correct sentence construction and composition. So we will begin today with Chapter One."

He then stumbled and stuttered his way through the hour, gave us our homework assignment and exited the room. What is wrong with the man, why is he so nervous? Sue Ann began to laugh, (she seemed to know all about men) and said, "Mr. Hunter is very uncomfortable because he is in a room with only girls who are young and pretty and I can prove it. Next week I will sit up front with my skirt a little above my knees and flirt with him and you all can observe".

Next Thursday we were eagerly waiting for Mr. Hunter's arrival. Sue Ann was seated in the front row. The professor arrived sweating and blushing. After a few minutes Sue Ann said in a very sexy voice, "Mr. Hunter, you have such a nice accent, are you from Britain?" Could anyone perspire or blush more? He could barely get the words out, "Indeed I am English, so sweet of you to notice." He proceeded to give us a case history about how he ended up in our area and that was the end of that English lesson.

Sue Ann was right, now we had his number, so to speak. All we needed to do to get Mr. Hunter off track was to sit Sue Ann up front.

The following week after a short exchange with Sue Ann, Mr. Hunter began telling us the weirdest, strangest stories full of sex, lies, greed and murder most vile. These tales made the hair on the back of your neck stand up. He said they were famous Greek myths. What would our teaching staff think if they walked in? It was vastly entertaining, even more racy then that shocking book, Peyton Place, that was passed around our high school classrooms with certain pages marked.

The weeks went by and we couldn't wait until Thursday. Sentence structure became very interesting. We were given strange sentences to identify parts of speech and diagram. One was, "Olympia was at odds with his father because he wanted to have sex with his mother." Whatever happened to "the quick young fox jumped over the lazy old dog"? We giggled and went to work. Never was English so much fun.

Our last assignment was to compose a short story. O dear, what to write about? Would we receive a good grade if we wrote about mundane things or would we dare to write something Mr. Hunter would enjoy? As a group, we decided to pick mundane. There was always a chance someone would obtain access to our papers and Mr. Hunter would be toast.

All in all, that English class was an interesting diversion, thanks to Sue Ann. The tedious journey through nouns, adjectives and verbs turned into an unexpected, very informative adventure into the seamy side of life.

Believe it or not, Mr. Hunter seemed pleased with most of our short stories. Wonders never cease! Too soon, it was all over and we were left to invent our own entertainment. One thing was very obvious, our English professor was no English gentleman.

Chapter 16
Getting it Done
Rachel

Pressure is mounting to get everything done this morning on 2 South, the absolutely worst floor. I am assigned a four patient ward down at the end of the hall. All this involves the taking of vital signs, personal care including bed baths, linen changes, serving breakfast, feeding the patients if necessary and even cleaning the steel-topped bedside stand with a brush and Bon Ami – no streaks allowed. Last but not least – charting. The clinical instructors will check our work during and after we are finished. They are so particular even the pillow cases are checked to see if the open side is turned towards the windows and not the entry door. Like who really cares?

One of the major problems is there are never enough clean sheets and we don't have time to wait for laundry delivery. So I was over here at 6 a.m. hiding sheets so I could make my beds and finish on time.

This morning my four patients are men, so that means I must round up an orderly to "finish" the bath and if any of the men need help with the urinal or bed pan I must again find the orderly. There is only one on duty on this floor so I hope last night's medicine nurse skipped the Milk of Magnesia.

Mr. Smith is very ill, but such a nice patient and so uncomplaining. He has pneumonia and coughs a lot. He must be turned every two hours because it is such an effort for him to move in bed and believe it or not, people can develop terrible ulcers in pressure areas such as heels and tail bones if not moved frequently. I certainly don't want that to happen to Mr. Smith.

We are required to write up at least four case studies every month and Mr. Smith will be one of my four cases. This report must include diagnosis, treatment, medications and prognosis. Another assignment is a medication report to be given once a week during morning report at shift change.

Mr. Sotherly is another patient. He had been in an auto accident and has a fractured leg (femur) which is in a cast beginning at his upper thigh and going all the way to his ankle. He has been here almost four weeks. Such a gossip he is, knows all the politics going on in the whole unit. He told me this morning that one of the night nurses (name included) is sweet on one of the married doctors. According to Mr. Sotherly, the doctor is paying a little too much attention to her. For someone who is unable to leave his bed, he seems to know everything. He told me he often pretends to be asleep and the nurses just talk away. He also told me some of the students skip a lot of their work and some days no one even helps him with his bath, they just get him a pan of water. I looked on his chart and "assistance with bath" is always charted. I wouldn't think of taking a chance like that.

The two other patients don't know they are in this world, so they are complete care. Both have urinary catheters and urine drips into large jugs under their beds. I gag every time I have to empty those. No doubt we are helping the sick but it is hard work that is never really over. Once in a while we are able to help other students who have particularly difficult assignments. I would like to see a student helper walk in my room this morning. Mr. Southerly was called to x-ray and I was there for thirty minutes. I did manage to get finished in time to chart, but in walked the doctors and they were off with my charts, so it's back over here at 3 p.m. when classes are over, no rest today.

Tomorrow is Friday. Hurray! Hurray! I will be going home, never did that word sound so lovely as it does at this moment. Home cooked meals, a long hot soak in the tub and sleep in my own bedroom. Heaven couldn't be sweeter. Mother always cooks one of my favorite meals and this weekend it will be homemade bread with raspberry jam and chicken noodle soup and that's just Friday evening. I drag all my dirty laundry home and she does that too. I'll not tell her how difficult it really is here. She is so pleased that I am in nursing school and I know she prays for me everyday. Complaining with other students is stepped up every time we get together and I do my share. However, I don't want to worry Mother by complaining at home.

There is so much to learn and I must say it helps to be working with the patients. The "on hands" aids in understanding the book work. No matter how busy the day or how discouraged I become, I just think of Mr. Smith who appreciates everything I do for him and today he called me his angel. Just his smile can make my heart lighter and I believe it just might be worth it after all.

Chapter 17
Specialties, How are they Special?
Grace

Posted on the bulletin board in the downstairs hall right next to the mail boxes is "The List." Everyone is talking about going into the specialties. We begin this rotation in alphabetical order (of course) and the first one is surgery. I'm a "C" so I go in with the very first group. The older students have already scared us to death with their horror stories. They say of all the specialties, surgery is the worst. We will be there for a long eight weeks and scrub for the doctors, which means we hand them instruments, sponges and suture while they are operating. Some of the surgeons are patient and helpful but a few don't like student nurses learning on their time and can be very nasty, especially that red-headed one we call Red Hood. He hates students, yells and curses them in front of other doctors and nurses. I am terrified! Well, I looked at "The List" and sure enough I start next Monday. Going along with me are seven others and they are just as upset as I. No hiding in the background, we will be right up there on the firing line.

If we survive surgery then follows Obstetrics with labor, delivery, new baby nursery, formula room and floor duty caring for new mothers. Next we go to Pediatrics, then Cysto, Diet Kitchen and Emergency Room. Our last specialty is three months away at Summer Meadows State Mental Hospital learning Psychiatric Nursing.

I'm not sure I want to continue down this road with so many challenges! Another two and one half years, it sounds like forever. At least we will be in different areas and maybe if I get through all this I will be able to decide where in nursing I would like to work.

Pauline gets a break. She will be following me in the next group and will have the benefit of learning from all my mistakes.

The older students pass down their survival lists by mouth. For surgery they suggest the following:

1 - Always look humble and don't disagree with any of the graduate nurses.
2 - Don't voice your opinions or suggest improvements.
3 - Be very, very careful that you don't contaminate yourself or your sterile field in the operating room.
4 – Learn name and use of all the instruments so you can hand the correct ones to the doctor when asked.
5 - Be on time. Never be late or you are sure to be assigned to scrub

in "Red Hood's" room.

6 - Be sure you keep a correct count of all sponges and needles you hand to the doctor. They will want to kill you if they are ready to close (sew up) and the count is wrong.

7 - Don't faint at the sight of blood or seeing the insides of people.

8 - Be happy to help clean up the room after surgeries are over.

9 - Don't ever complain about being tired or how difficult your day has been within the surgery staff's hearing.

10 - If you are working in the supply center always, always stop at the dining hall and write down the lunch menu. The staff will have a collective faint if you forget!

11 - If you are assigned to preps (shaving patient's operative sites), do them well. Don't leave one hair standing even if the razors are as dull as dirt. The bright operation room lights will reveal all attached hairs.

12 - When you are on "Surgical Call", on nights and weekends, don't complain, but be prompt when called, even if it is 4 a.m. and you already scrubbed for a case at midnight.

13 - Pray every morning before "going over" and celebrate when the day is over, one more day only forty seven to go.

I suppose we'll be getting unwritten advice lists concerning the other specialties too. I wonder if Mother will let me come home? No there is no use asking. She has paid up and again, there is no refund.

Well, I must get my shoes shined, my hose washed, put my hair up in bobby pins and get my uniform ready for tomorrow. Also, I need to finish studying for a huge Medical Surgical test on "The cause and symptoms of circulatory system failure and how can it be corrected?" I need to know about all this because I think my own circulatory system is about to fail. Monday morning will be here before I can turn around. Am I anxious? Am I scared? Is the Pope Catholic? Is rain wet?

Chapter 18
We Have No Money!
Jill

My pockets are empty. I'm waiting for money from Daddy. He paid my tuition for the first year, $225, payment for uniforms, books, college tuition, library fees and bus transportation to the college. I had saved some money from my summer job at the 5 and 10 cent store, but it's all gone now. Room and board is provided (we give the hospital lots of free labor), but there are personal expenses, such as stockings (white), deodorant, shampoo, soap, tooth brushes, tooth paste, soap etc., etc.

It's amazing how far you can stretch a jar of deodorant and how there is no such thing as an empty tube of toothpaste. I have used baking soda and salt for toothpaste on occasion, terrible tasting stuff. Great care is needed with those white stockings, I have nail polish ready to stop all runners. Once I didn't have any clear polish and had to use pink. Thank goodness the runner was in my shoe.

Also, I ride the bus to Grandma's house on the weekend and the fare costs me twenty cents just one way. My mother died from cancer when I was fifteen and she was thirty four years old. When she died, our family as we had known it died too. My older brother joined the Air Force, my dad went away to work and my younger brother and I went to live with my Grandmother. I miss having a family of my own. Buying any extra food is out of the question. I do try and save five cents a day for a Coke from the machine downstairs, only one. I believe I could drink six Cokes every day, they taste so good! I am always hungry! Nothing is refused at meals, even food I would never eat such as broccoli, Brussels sprouts, and cooked cabbage, ugh! The desserts, lovely! If ever I'm able to earn my own money, I swear I'm going to buy food, glorious food – and lots of candy bars, cookies, cakes, ice cream and so on.

Reva doesn't have any money either. In fact, she worked and earned her own money to pay all her own fees. After helping her mother, giving her five dollars a week while working and still at home, she exhausted all the funds she was planning to use for personal expenses. Her dad doesn't have work all the time and it is tough going for her family. About once a month she receives a little money from her mother.

The reason Reva came to nursing school was because it cost less than college. She finished one semester at Morgan, then her dream of being a teacher was over. She couldn't pay the tuition and her parents just couldn't do it for her. She worked for eight months at an office job and then came to Wayside, the cheaper alternative for some kind of higher education.

Reva and I love to go to the shops downtown. We look at all the lovely dresses, shoes, and hats. There is a wonderful jewelry store and we linger at the windows and hope someday we will own at least one diamond. I hear they are a girl's best friend. The shop windows at Christmas are beautiful. The department stores are all a glitter and oh, the beautiful winter coats! I saw a white one that was to die for. Of course, neither Reva nor I are able to add to our meager wardrobes. Thank goodness we have uniforms! I suppose I am poor but so is most everyone here and there is little talk of money. Sometimes when the smoking girls get together I think I might like to smoke too. It looks so sophisticated, like in the movies. But no money for cigarettes, that's for sure.

Once in a while I can gather together enough coins for a movie. There is a theater across town that costs only ten cents. It is not your upper class place, torn seats, dirty rest rooms, all in all very worn out looking. People call it the "Bug House." I haven't met up with any fleas yet and they play wonderful movies (not the fleas). Such fun! Somehow I feel rich just sitting there watching the movie stars. I love the musicals, all those beautiful outfits and oh how they can dance!

Great News! Someone down the hall just received a box from home. Lindsay is sharing cookies and fudge! And yes, look there is a letter from Daddy. I think I will buy Lindsay, Reva and me a Coke. It's like I received pennies from Heaven. I have a twenty dollar bill!

Chapter 19
Capping - Uneasy is the Head that Wears the Crown
Katie

Today we receive our caps after seven months of training and yes, it really is a big deal or should I say a big tease? If I flunk out or quit, I will never be able to actually wear it. Thirty-seven of us have made the cut. Our families were notified and the ceremony is to be held at a high school in town. After today we will be wearing our white bibs too. They attach to our aprons. So we will go on duty looking like we might know something, our uniforms complete with Wayside's cap on our heads. After graduation (pray we make it) we will be allowed to add a black velvet stripe to our caps. This is just fine for now, I never dreamed I could make it this far and no matter what they throw at me, I am determined to finished.

Programs for the ceremony have our names printed on them along with our class motto, class poem, class prayer and order of service. There will be music played and for one week we have been trying to memorize the Nightingale Pledge. We are to recite this together. Our teachers, clinical instructors and supervisors will be there including the great Mrs. Rivers.

After everyone is seated we will walk down the aisles and onto the stage wearing our present uniforms with bibs and all holding unlit candles. After a few prayers and songs we will have caps placed on our heads and our candles lit. Here's hoping there isn't a fire. We will then all receive a Gideon Bible and say that pledge. Won't my dad and stepmother be proud? My sister, Della, will also be there with a scattering of aunts and uncles.

We must all look very solemn and dedicated and I guess pretend that emptying bedpans, dressing wounds, giving enemas and other rather distasteful procedures are really very noble and somehow very satisfying. Well, I can pretend with the best of them and everyone looks so pretty. Who would believe that yesterday someone threw up all over Susie and some old man pinched Ava as she was bending over to straighten his bedside stand? I could say that today we are happy hypocrites.

Butter wouldn't melt in Mrs. Rivers' mouth and she smiles (really) as we walk in one by one. I expect her at any time to stand up and tell Ida to go pin up her hair or tell Karen her shoes have a smudge on them. Of course, she wouldn't dare. People are watching and it's all sweetness and light. She has a speech all prepared about how proud she is of each one of us for how much we have accomplished so far and what great things we are going to contribute to the cause of medicine. All of this from the lady who just last week wanted to toss three girls out the door for going over for evening snacks wearing their shorts. "Proper attire must be worn to pick up cheese and bread." Her very words! After finishing her remarks we all smiled and clapped. Her frown returned when we did so poorly with the Nightingale Pledge. The first few lines went well but only some remembered the last part. What was old Florence going on about anyhow?

In closing statements we were told that, of course, there would be challenges ahead but we must keep on keeping on with our duties and studies, forging ahead so someday we would be a credit to Wayside and anywhere else we chose to go in our professional careers.

Congratulations and happy faces all around. Yes, it is a great day. Maybe there will be more such days ahead. It feels good to have a little praise heaped on, unusual too. And our families so are proud. Dad smiled and smiled. My stepmother even cried. My sister who is eight stuck out her tongue and said, "Congratulations Sis." Aunt Betty and Uncle Albert gave me a card with five whole dollars in it. I kept my cap on the rest of the evening. I would have worn it to bed but I would have messed it up, so I laid it carefully on my side of the dresser. Staring at it, I hated to turn off the light. Mrs. Stone blinked the hall lights, so that was that, but just think tomorrow I will wear my cap to the hospital for the first time. I love my cap!

All and all, everything went as planned and we made it through and I must say we are all feeling a little prideful this day. We hadn't wiped all those bottoms for nothing after all.

NIGHTINGALE PLEDGE

I solemnly pledge myself before God and in the presence of this assembly to pass by life in purity and to practice my profession faithfully.

I will abstain from whatever is deleterious and mischievous, and will not take or knowingly administer any harmful drug.

I will do all in my power to maintain and elevate the standards of my profession, and will hold in confidence all personal matters committed to my keeping and all family affairs coming to my knowledge in the practice of my profession.

With loyalty will I endeavor to aid the physician in his work and devote myself to the welfare of those committed to my care.

CLASS MOTTO
"One step at a time,
but always forward."

Chapter 20
Medicine Girl
Feona

I have no life. Here I am, 6:30 in the morning, standing at the nurses' station on 2 South with about twenty other hospital staff listening to how fifty three sick people spent the night. They lie in beds in rooms up and down the hall. Not only that, two are actually in beds in the hall waiting for someone to be discharged or die so they can go into a room. I didn't know there were that many sick folks in the whole state. Everyone around me looks a little dazed and some are actually yawning. I feel like someone hit me over the head with a rock or something. The pain starts at my forehead and travels right through my head to the back of my neck. Ask me why I ever came here? I could strangle my sister, Joyce. She should be here instead of me. Today I continue learning how to medicate the entire hall. The clinical instructor will be with me one on one the whole morning. Thank goodness it's Miss Kirby.

The medicine room is a little closet across from the nurses' station. Shelves with sliding doors line the walls. There are boxes of pills, bottles of weird looking liquids, trays, needles and syringes, a sink that could use a little of that Bon Ami, a sterilizer, spoons, and a locked cabinet that holds all the narcotics and barbiturates. All a bit overwhelming. I believe I am claustrophobic and I think I am having an anxiety attack (we just learned about those last week). One of the second year students started screaming when she received a call from delivery room, her fourth baby that evening was about to be born. She yelled and hollered saying she couldn't stand one more screaming mother and squealing baby. Her roommate told her to pull herself together and quit acting like a banshee. Tomorrow she would be off call and then she could scream all she wanted, but right now she better get her shoes on and head out. Anxiety attack over!

Well, I guess my situation is a little better than that. This shouldn't be too hard. Nurses give out meds all the time and most look rather calm carrying around their trays. But what if I give someone the wrong medicine? There is much talk of incident reports and trips to Mrs. River's office. One student was "kicked out" because she gave the wrong person insulin; she (the patient) went into some kind of shock and almost died! What if I kill someone! These people take pills all day long for all sorts of things and some can't even answer when you call their name or say "yes" to someone else's name. Miss Kirby keeps saying "check the wrist band, check the wrist band, but hurry, you haven't finished the "bids" (twice a day) and it's almost time for the "tids", (three times a day), and then there are "qids" (four times a day). Be sure and check the medicine cards to see if there is a discontinue date. You also must make sure the patient actually swallows the pills. Some might try to spit them back out. Some may even refuse and you must try to convince them how important it is for their health that they comply."

"The cards must be separated and every medication given must be charted. Never lose a card and always return them to the correct box for the next dose." Thank goodness the cards are different colors for times given. There are small paper cups for pills, but all liquid medicine must be measured into little glass cups which then must be washed and sterilized after use. On and on it goes and we have not even mentioned the "prns" (give when necessary) meds that can interrupt ones well laid out delivery plans. "Hartman, Mrs. Kidman in 220 needs her pain medication "stat" (immediately)." Are you kidding? I'm down the end of the hall passing out the "tids." Every narcotic and sleeping pill dispensed from the locked cupboard must be recorded on a special sheet with the patient's name and time given (double charting). At the end of each shift the count must be correct or the whole place goes crazy. Also, you must check the patient's chart to see if they haven't asked for the pain medication too soon. If the order is every four hours it better not be just three hours and twenty minutes. One of my fellow students told me a patient threw a bed pan (empty, thank goodness) at her when she walked in the room with pain medication ten minutes late.

We haven't even discussed injections (shots) that will be taught another day. The medicine nurse also gives all of these; insulin, antibiotics, shots for pain and on and on. My headache is getting worse as I go with Miss Kirby to begin setting up. She is very patient and kind. It must be a real chore working with such ignorant girls. I wonder what her head feels like? Just think, I could probably be working at the paper mill cutting paper sheets. I couldn't kill anyone there, just cut off my own fingers.

Grace has already done medicines and she assured me that once you get the hang of it, it's not as difficult as imagined, it even gets to be routine and at least you don't have to do a.m. cares. She is a calm one. After working all day, she looks like she is just walked on the floor to begin. A nice contrast I make, uniform dirty, sweating, hair flying around and exhaustion written all over my face. I really don't believe anyone has thrown up on her yet. Of course, being a medicine nurse is just a walk in the park for her. No anxiety attacks and a medicine mistake – never! This is not envy, I just wish I could be like her and she could be even better. Just another day at the office. "Really Hartman, get those cards lined up. We haven't all day, it is 7:45 and time for the 8 a.m.'s." Off we go, wish me luck!

Chapter 21
Needles – Not Just Used for Sewing
Jo Jo

Interesting stuff – how to put medicine inside a body other than orally (by mouth). Mrs. Summers began our instruction by letting us practice sticking needles into oranges. The technique for filling the syringes takes a lot of practice too, all air bubbles must be removed and one must be very accurate with the dosage. The wrong dose could be bad news and air in the syringe could cause an embolism (air) that might be fatal, ominous thoughts. I always hated those shots we had to get at school and before we came in here we had to have another round. Now here was my chance. I will be on the other end of the needle. Some shots are given deep in the muscle, usually in the buttocks with a long needle. Others can be given in the upper arm with shorter needles. Some meds are given right under the skin, (subq). Diabetics get their insulin into fatty tissue like the abdomen. Where, how and when to give the medicine will be written on the medicine cards. The needles, of course, are of different lengths. When a patient receives lots of shots, the sites have to be rotated.

The syringes are made of glass and used over and over, cleaned and sterilized after each use. The needles are also reused and must be sterilized – the job of the medicine nurse. Both are kept in a sterile container in the medicine room. There is even a way to sharpen the dull ones. Needles sometimes after repeated use become dull and we can sharpen these with sand paper if we have time, if not they rake going in, not a happy thought. I am told that I must be very careful not to contaminate the needle and the skin must be wiped with alcohol before injection. We have been taught all this and I believe I am ready.

This morning, Mrs. Connor on 4 South is my clinical instructor and I will give my first shots. She uses the word "injections." I suppose that sounds more professional. So now I go injecting!

The patient, Mr. Powers, is a little suspicious as we walk in with the shot on a tray, the needle resting on a cotton ball soaked in alcohol. Coming in with the clinical instructor must have given him a clue. She asks him to turn on his side and explains to him that he is to receive his medication in the buttocks. This site must be carefully chosen because it is possible to hit a major nerve with the needle which could cause severe problems. That leg on that side could become paralyzed. Upper-outer quadrant – sounds like a spot on a baseball field.

I can do this, so why is my hand shaking? The needle looks really long and it must go deep and Mr. Power's skin isn't a bit like an orange! I paused and held my breath then stuck it in. Mr. Powers gave out a cry and said loudly, "This is her first time, isn't it? You just use us poor patients to practice on we are just guinea pigs and I wasn't even involved in the decision. A patient has no rights these days."

I was thoroughly put out. We do have to learn. Patients can be terribly uncooperative. Well, it was over and not as difficult as anticipated. Actually I liked it and even felt a feeling of power. I am the one with the needle, after all.

That day I gave ten more "injections." My last patient only complained a little so I guess I'm getting a little quicker and better at the actual administration (hey, I like that word). I'm administering medications, or should I say medications by injections, certainly a step up from emptying bed pans. Each shot must be recorded on the patient's chart, medication, time given, place given, etc. Charting is a pain, but we have been told patient's records are very important and everything must be written correctly. I wonder what happens to all those papers.

I'm actually looking forward to tomorrow and the rest of the week on needle brigade. I can't wait to do the IV thing, but that won't be until we are seniors. Is there something wrong with me, enjoying sticking needles into folks? Maybe, just maybe it is because I'm finally getting into something that isn't grunt work, needs some skill and is so nurse-like. Not just anyone can pull this off. One must be trained and have a lot of nerve. My goal is to be the "best gal with the needle."

Chapter 22
Germs, Germs are Everywhere
Pauline

We are learning clean technique and sterile technique in our Nursing Arts class. It seems there are all kinds of germs, unseen, whose goal is to kill every human being living. They keep trying to get inside and wreck havoc. The human body also has a fighting unit (white cells) that take up arms against germ invaders. A royal battle seems to be always going on and we are totally unaware. The purpose of all those painful childhood immunizations is just to put a little of those terrible germs inside so the body will more or less know the enemy and be ready to fight if a bunch of those little buggers find a way in.

In the meantime, everything is done to prevent invasion. Washing hands is so simple, but most important, because germs can be carried from one person to another. Also, they can be breathed in, so masks are necessary if the germs are airborne. I picture them riding around in tiny planes, flying up our noses as we inhale.

Mrs. Summers is teaching us how to prevent infection especially in surgery. Everything must be sterilized. This is done by boiling or cooking in large autoclaves burning all those germs alive. Apparently any open wound is a door in for sure and great care must be given to block their entry. If the germs do get in, there are many different medications now discovered that can do much to help the white cells inside to win the battle. Mrs. Summers explained how we as nurses could be agents of trouble. How clean is clean? "Wipe areas only with clean cloths, wipe skin with alcohol before injections, wear masks if you have cold symptoms, don't cough on anyone, get out of the way if anyone sneezes around you, always wear a clean uniform, always wipe from front to back when cleaning up after bed pan use, don't put anyone's bed pan in someone else's bedside stand, don't drink out of anyone else's cup, wash hands, wash hands, wash hands and on and on.

I believe I am getting germ phobia. The other day I picked up someone else's coke bottle by mistake and took a big drink. I almost threw up. Last week, while home, I was helping Mom make cookies and she almost knows nothing about germs. She used the dish cloth to wipe something off the floor and then wiped the table! Did my face turn green? Doesn't she realize we could all die just from things in the kitchen? Using the toilet is so scary – who was in there before me? I'm starting to carry around a bottle of alcohol and using it on toilet seats. I won't even wear my socks twice! Giving those awful enemas and douches – just think of the germs! My hands are red and sore, could all those little invaders who can't even be seen be trying to get in through my hang nails? The thought of kissing anyone on the lips is gross! Imagine the germs that would be transferred. My boyfriend doesn't understand the danger.

I talked all this over with some of the other students and they reminded me that we have lived all these years without knowing what is really going on with this particular unseen world and so far, so good. "Just do your best and quit worrying. There are lots of people working on this, scientists and all." That's easy for them to say. They don't have dreams about little multicolored demons trying to break down their skin barrier.

Well, that germ course is finally over and now we are on to Nutrition and Diet Therapy and are learning about all the foods that are bad for us. I'm thinking less about germs and worrying about fried foods and animal fat. Cakes, pies and candy bars are murder. Many health problems come from bad diets, like diabetes, a real killer. So now it's fruits and vegetables for me. Everything I like to eat is bad for me. I cut off all traces of fat; shun sugar, delicious but dangerous. Chocolate can cause acne and even artificial sweeteners can do one in. All intake must be carefully monitored, proteins, fats, carbohydrates to be counted, daily amounts of vitamins and minerals need to be considered, adequate and daily exercise to keep one fit and healthy. Yesterday, I broke down and ate a candy bar. How could I give in like that? I'm such a weakling.

I have almost forgotten about germs. There are more pressing concerns out there. In two weeks we will begin studying about strokes, heart failure and kidney disease. All terrible conditions that may be deadly. I'm surrounded by pitfalls and dead end streets. My roommate tells me she is concerned about my mental health. What! I can hardly wait to begin studying that subject! I need an escape! A good movie would be just the thing.

Chapter 23
Surgery – Working in Hell's Doorway
Reva

I've never seen anything quite like this. A whole prior unknown world with its own kings and queens, princesses and peasants, and I know who the peasants are. The queen in charge is a witch-like woman, grim and mean looking, could have been Snow White's stepmother. A poison apple is hidden somewhere, I just know it!

The place is full of people in costumes, all white. In the actual surgery rooms they look like a bunch of ghosts showing only their eyes.

Walking in that first day was an eye-opener. There were a lot of women in the hall and one was assigned to showing us around. There are six operating rooms, some for major and others for minor cases (what could be minor about being cut up?). We made the grand tour and I saw scrub sinks with nurses washing their arms and hands with soap and brushes. Then they went with their arms bent at the elbows into different rooms. There another nurse put robes on them, sterile gloves and masks. They are to scrub (assist) the surgeons by handing him sponges, needles, clamps and so on. We will begin to do this very thing in two days!

Mrs. Farley (Snow White's Stepmother) takes her head nurse position very seriously. She growls as she speaks and seems just plain weary of having to break in another bunch of green girls.

We observed all that first day, people being rolled in and out of rooms. They must have opened up ten that day. Children having tonsils extracted, a bloody business with the smell of ether dancing around the room, two hysterectomies, a few bone repairs, one foot amputee and several other opening ups.

Finally they are all finished the surgeries and a very large lady named Cooper (they call each other by last names), showed us the cleaning up routine. Each room must be returned with zeal to its pre-surgery state. Everything in the room washed off with antiseptic, instruments and needles are soaked in a stinking solution named Barb Parker and then they must be packed in sterile trays in perfect order. We will be doing this tomorrow going from room to room with Cooper. After that we will be on our own (while they have coffee and cigarettes in the nurses' room). However, they will inspect and all must be in tip top shape. I suppose the world would end if a drop of blood is missed or a needle is not in correct line.

Two mornings later at 6:30 a.m. we students are all here and start at the scrub sinks. You must begin at the upper arm and work down.

Ten minutes each arm with brush and soap. While we are scrubbing, the head nurse or assistant head nurse will call out – Flanagan A, Hartman E, and so on until all six rooms are assigned. The clinical nurse will be right beside us today. Poor Katie will be scrubbing for Old Red Hood who screams and curses at everyone through the whole procedure. All are idiots except him. He is especially brutal to the students. He must think the worst he treats us the better we will turn out. If I were Katie, I would be having a heart attack. I'm glad I will be assisting one of the nicer doctors for a gall bladder removal. Nevertheless I am feeling like I am coming apart inside, my first surgery case.

It's very hot in the room and I'm already sweating as they roll our victim in and move her over on the operating table and start covering her up until only her abdomen shows. The anesthesiologist (the sleep maker) sits at the top of the table and starts pumping up things and gets out a rubber mask with a long tube attached and slaps it over the patient's mouth. If I didn't know better I would think I was somewhere in outer space. The surgeon walks in, looks at an x-ray up on the wall, has his gown, gloves, and mask put on and looks over at me and says "Well, I understand this is the day the new bunch starts. Welcome! Today we will be extracting this woman's gall bladder", and then went on to explain why it was necessary. Apparently she will be in much better health without this particular part. Finally, after about an hour of messing around inside, he pulls out a very strange looking thing – that looks like a pink gray worm and a nurse comes by with a jar and the doctor plops it in. Now he is ready to start sewing the lady's stomach shut. A count is taken of the sponges that were laid on the floor in little bloody rows by the circulating nurse. "Sponge count correct, Doctor," she shouts. The closing begins as I hand over needle and thread (suture) on a needle holder to the surgeon and he stitches everything closed but the last skin layer. "Needle count correct, Doctor," is shouted out and skin sutures are applied. No one wants to deal with the consequences if any of these foreign objects are left inside. Dressings and adhesive tape are slapped on and it is all over. The patient is moved onto a cart and out she goes. The whole bloody business was tension filled and very nerve wracking and to think I just wanted to be a teacher!! Then I was told to take off my operating gown and go scrub up again. In thirty minutes we will be doing an appendectomy. Patients aren't called by their names but by the procedures. "It is that hysterectomy here yet? We are just finishing the second T & A today. The amputation is ready in room D." What a place! Why would anyone want to do this?

Today begins my third week and they hate me here. I don't understand it. I have followed all commands and haven't once complained within ear shot of the staff. Feona told me (they love her), "They are all just jealous. You don't have a humble look about you, in fact, you look regal in

51

your scrubs. They think you might know more than they do." Of course, that's impossible. Never was I here before.

Just yesterday Feona and I were in the autoclave room. I was over closing a window and she opened the autoclave to remove some surgical packs. The clinical instructor walked in and started shouting at me "Flannigan, you opened the autoclave before the pressure was down. Do you want to blow a hole in the hospital wall? You are nothing but trouble." Feona started to protest but Cooper just went on and on. I thought smoke would come out of her ears. She shouted again, "If you are so careless again you will be making out an incident report and off to Mrs. Rivers you will go (they never call her just Rivers). Now get out of here and start cleaning room 'F'."

One thing is for sure, I will never ever choose to work in surgery. These ladies are demons on wheels. I don't think they even like each other. In fact, I heard one telling the 'queen' that another nurse was trying to get out of work excusing herself by taking multiple trips to the nurses' lounge when it was time to clean rooms and put out surgical packs for the next morning. They are always complaining about each other to get closer to the 'queen'. Who would want to live in this world? I can't wait to escape, only four more weeks. They say you can get used to hanging if you hang long enough, but I would never get used to it here. My last day calls for a huge celebration, I'll walk out Hell's doorway rejoicing!

Chapter 24
Is July Really Here?
Lindsay

Three whole weeks at home! Could I be more homesick? My suitcase is out but I can't decide what to pack so I'm packing everything except those dreadful text books and uniforms. Mother will have two of my three weeks off work and we are going to the "River."

I love the "River." We have a big house there and it is surrounded by Trees, wild flowers and beautiful grasses. The "River" is about 50 feet from the back door and it winds around, through deep banks with trees hanging over. We wade in the shallow places and down the way is a deep area where we all swim. Daddy put a rope on one of those hanging trees and we can swing out and drop off. Such fun! I learned to swim at the "River."

We go for hikes and gather flowers for the table and Mother cooks all those fresh garden vegetables. Summer is truly the best time for eating. My favorite is corn on the cob, dripping with butter.

Nights are lovely! We sit on the porch and watch the lightening bugs and later listen to all those summer night sounds. We light up a bon fire and toast marshmallows, tell stories, sing songs and hymns.

Getting away from here will be a much anticipated break. There is little encouragement here or praise for jobs well done, instead there is lots of criticism. It seems I can't do anything that pleases the supervisors. Also, I never knew there could be such sadness. Some of my patients were terribly sick and a few never got to go home. I believe one can really feel a broken heart. It is rewarding to be able to help, but I need an escape for a while. I swear I'm not going to think about sickness, rules, classes, tests, new procedures, surgery or any other scary things ahead for three whole weeks.

We do have some good times here, all is not gloom and doom, or work and worry. Some of the girls have an uncanny ability to find humor in the most trying circumstances and we laugh a lot. One of the girls asked one of the doctors (he was in his white surgical scrubs), mistaking him for an orderly to please come and take Mr. White off the bedpan, She said, "Where have you been hiding after all?" The doctor told her, "I've been a little busy. I just finished an appendectomy." She was mortified. Doctors are gods around here.

I enjoy playing tennis and going for walks. We also, when we have free time, watch the one T.V. down in the lounge. Not many nurses can get in that room at a time, but if I can find a seat, I watch whatever happens to be on.

The other evening a few of us walked down to the ice cream shop and got a huge cone, three scoops for five cents and then went on to see a movie, "Farewell to Arms," a real tear jerker. Those short breaks really help. Nothing, however, can beat going home and I do make it home most weekends, but I have to spend time studying for the next week's tests. So many subjects, some are behind us but more coming up. It's like going through some kind of gauntlet. Some of the doctors will be teaching us come September. They do this without pay, so I am told. Quite nice of them. Many act like they want to help us become good nurses and are very encouraging. Yesterday I had to follow one around with the dressing cart while he changed bandages on surgical wounds and removed sutures from some. He was very kind. Of course some are not. They act like they are very important and we should all scrape and bow. Would you believe when one walks into the nurses' station we all must stand up?

I can forget it all for three blissful weeks. Our relatives will be coming to visit. Some of my cousins will be with us at the "River." Mother, bless her, has invited some of my high school friends. Talking about high school and boyfriends will be great fun! Those days were great, now that I look back. My whole world has changed, except for home.

Dear God, please let the days go by slowly. I want to savor every minute. Going home, going home, I'll be going home. Mother's there, Father's there, all the friends I've known.

SECOND YEAR

September 1957 – September 1958

Chapter 25
Obstetrics – Easier Said Than Done
Grace

It's September of our second year, one down and two to go. This will be a busy year, starting this month we will begin our classes in Obstetrical Nursing, 60 credit hours. Some of the head nurses from this department will be our teachers, also some of the OB doctors.

Our first OB doctor is a new physician who just came to the area this year. The first day he walked in our classroom and sat down at the desk, we all perked up. His name is Dr. Fungi, dark, handsome and young. I was fascinated with his eyes. I suppose he is Italian, but he has beautiful blue eyes that actually twinkle. He looked us over and said "I suppose you are wondering about my name. I received much ridicule in my growing up years and thought seriously about changing it, but it is our family name and I'm sticking with it." His voice was musical. Here was a doctor worth listening to.

He began his lecture by saying, "I feel like the man with a harem. I know what to do but I don't know where to start." Much laughter and we all relaxed. This was getting very interesting. His subject was pregnancy and delivery. We were ready to listen and learn. I know a little about this because I used to hide behind the door to our kitchen at home when my mother and her sisters would speak of such things while having tea in the afternoon.

Dr. Fungi was talking about pregnancy, it being a very normal condition only lasting nine months. Not long when one considers that an elephant is pregnant for two years.

What I heard from behind the door at home.

Aunt Betsy – "I thought those months would never be over. I threw up everything for the first three, had terrible problems with fainting the next three and my last three, my stomach was so huge I couldn't see my feet, my ankles looked like tree trunks." Sleep was impossible, I just couldn't get comfortable. Would this misery ever end?

Then Dr. Fungi spoke of beginning labor and with the first child this could last many rather long hours with contractions coming at distant intervals.

Aunt Ida – "When I started having those first pains, I felt like finally the time was here and I couldn't wait for it to be over. They hurt! I also remember thinking, 'I don't want to do this today but there is no stopping a moving train.'"

Dr. Fungi – "The second stage of labor contractions aren't too strong but continue to become more regulated and the soon-to-be mother can begin timing them and packing her suitcase."

Aunt Mildred – "The pains made me sit up and take notice, I can tell you. They started at my back and came around to my front. It felt like a giant cramp, extremely uncomfortable. I told Charles to throw my suitcase in the car and head out to Wayside."

Dr. Fungi – "The last stage of labor becomes rather intense with the contractions lasting longer and at more frequent intervals. Now it is necessary to begin the preparation for delivery. At the beginning of this stage the patient should be given an enema and have a surgical prep. The delivery nurse will do an exam to see how much the cervix is dilated and some mild medicine for pain may be given."

Aunt Betsy – "Well, I can tell you when the pains were getting closer they began to feel like someone was ripping out my insides and the nurse came in with a razor. Is she kidding? Couldn't' she have done this three hours ago when there was a rest in between? What, an enema? These people have an inside track on torture. After all that a nurse started doing exams, pouring some freezing liquid over me and hollering out things like "She is only three "cms" (centimeters), this will take a while." Both ends of my body were involved because I started to throw up. A nurse assured me that this was normal and the nausea would pass."

Dr. Fungi – "When the patient is six to eight "cms", she will be transferred from the labor room to the delivery room. She will be placed in the birth position and after a few rather hard contractions and an episiotomy (a scissors cut at the delivery sight) if necessary, the baby will be delivered, cord cut, placenta delivered and episiotomy sutured. Then the new mother will be transferred to OB floor and the baby to New Born Nursery."

Aunt Ida – "Only a woman could survive this ordeal, the human race would cease if men were having babies. I hated Joe. In fact, I believed I hollered that out loud. My legs were up in those strange looking things and the pains were body breaking. I thought I was dying for sure. The doctor was calmly humming a tune and asking the time. He said in two hours he was due at the golf course. Then he said, "Oh yes, I do believe the little one is indeed on the way out, hand me the scissors." Well, that was the topper, the baby pushing out and him coming at me with scissors. I hollered my protests but of course they were ignored. "Now push down, dearie, just one more of those contractions and the baby will be here." Joe is a dead man if I get out of here alive. The doctor said, "Well, here she is, a sweet little girl and very healthy looking, lovely dear thing. Hand me those clamps and we will just sit here and wait for the placenta. This is almost over and in good time too, I was beginning to think I would miss my tee time."

"After I was all sewed up and my legs returned to a normal position and a brief look at my little Nelly, they moved me to a moving cart and out of that dreadful room."

"I arrived at my room and was helped over to a bed with an actual mattress." The nurse said, "Now dearie, you will be able to rest for several days here before you take darling baby home. We will check you frequently for bleeding and pin on a breast binder since you are going to be a bottle feeder. The nursery nurse will be here in about three hours with your baby so you can begin feedings. If you need anything for pain, let us know." Well, the terrible pain was over, except for a burning sensation at the delivery site. Did a truck run over me? I am so exhausted! I will never, ever, ever go through this again."

Well, one can learn a lot eavesdropping and I wanted to raise my handand ask dear Dr. Fungi if he ever had a baby, but I hadn't the nerve. I looked over at Reva, maybe she would ask the question. But no, she is silent. Everyone looks as if it is no big deal, but I know the truth.

So much for our first class with Dr. Fungi, next time he will talk about complications of pregnancy and delivery. Apparently things could be worse than mother and her sisters had experienced.

I just want to get out of this classroom and hit the shower, roll my hair, polish my shoes and skip dinner. I snuck in a few sandwiches from home. They are waiting for me in my room (two demerits if caught). I'm really tired after being on duty for four hours and then class with Dr. Fungi. Thank Goodness, tomorrow is Friday!

Chapter 26
The Writing on the Wall
Katie

This place is absolutely obsessed with checking up on everyone. There is room check every single night at lights out, room check every week for neatness and cleanliness, check on anyone who might be "campused" (they might have the nerve to sneak out), and even check up on whether anyone is checking up.

They have lists at the hospital for when you actually perform some procedure, such as bed baths, enemas, douches, wound dressings, catherizations, medication administration, urine check for diabetes, collection of outputs and charting, etc., etc. These lists must be somewhere filling up rooms with paper. But what I would really like to find out is what they do with those monthly reports.

At the end of each month a report sheet goes up on the bulletin board in the hallway of the nurses' home. On it is a list of all our names and we are to fill beside our names certain information for some apparently very nosy person or persons. We must list the number of case studies and the medication reports we have completed, what specialty we are currently in, any sick days (to be made up, of course), our weight (believe it or not), and last but not least, the date of our LMP (last menstrual period.) Really? Where are these reports taken and who reads them? Are they compared from month to month? What would be done if there is a sudden increase or decrease in weight and what about the timing between the LMP? Who in their right mind would dare to omit the date of her LMP if she didn't have one? There have been a few girls in the past (I'm told) who became pregnant while here and were quickly "kicked out" as soon as their condition became evident. If one could hide it until the last six months and have a hurry up wedding you might be home free. Most of the girls have boyfriends, but I don't know of any girls that are that serious. A few of us know about Amy. She is secretly married and she freaks out every month, sweating it out until her MP (menstrual period) shows up. So far, so good.

It seems we are all members of some secret club and have all banded together, not letting those in charge know any information about us. We stick behind any and all rule breakers, the great cover-uppers.

We even go so far as to open the locked hall doors to let someone in after hours, especially on weekends. Jewell, a senior, wanted to stay out later with her guy because he was leaving for the Army. Most of us would risk it all to let her in. She rolled up some covers in her bed to fool Mrs.

Stone at room check. Sometimes a "campused" girl is off campus for something important and we pretend we don't know where she is if someone higher up comes looking. Oh, we have our methods for protecting one another for sure. There is a lot of tension and stress and we do get on one another's nerves with this close living together, but we stick together in regards to the important things. Occasionally there is a problem with competing boyfriends, so we make up excuses on the telephone if one calls and the girl is out with another boy.

I'm not sure how this all happened it seems to have come out of nowhere. We protect our own. We are more relaxed around each other too. I remember when we first got here we took pains to look our best when leaving our rooms. Now we just let it all hang out, so to speak. If our hair is messed up or we don't have on lipstick, or we are in our worst outfit, or have had no new clothes for months and months, it's all okay. Like some kind of weird family, we have become very comfortable with each other.

About the breaking of rules, just last week two girls went off campus when we were told no one could leave in the afternoon for some dumb reason. Reva and Jill decided to go anyhow. Who could possibly find out? However, Mrs. Walker, one of the assistant housemothers, thought she saw two students in one of the shops downtown. She passed the information on to Miss Walls and she began to grill us the next day in class. Saying "Will the guilty ones please stand?" No one stood. "Okay, will someone please give me the names?" No one spoke. "Oh, come now, someone in here knows who deliberately disobeyed." All were silent. She became quite angry, shouting and threatening. Silence! She finally gave up and no demerits were given.

Sticking together for survival is our real class motto. It suits me, I wouldn't want it any other way. This is no place to live in isolation. Since we are all in the same boat, we will paddle together. How else will we make it through the rapids ahead?

Chapter 27
M-S Nursing – No End in Sight
Lindsay

For eighteen years I have been walking around in this body without realizing how intricate and complex it is. Medical-Surgical Nursing separates all the systems for individual study and then goes on to teach how they are all intertwined and work together. Amazing stuff, one could just take one system and study it for an entire lifetime. Then we learn the many ways these systems can be compromised through infection, injury, disease and age. All is a bit overwhelming and very difficult to keep straight in my mind. My whole life is filled with studying, tests and hospital duty.

Mrs. Caskey teaches this course. She is a good teacher and her tests are always based on exactly what she teaches. No surprises! If I pay attention, take good notes and study every night, I should pass.

We are now studying the Endocrine System with all its mysterious glands and secretions, hard to get your mind around. One day Mrs. Caskey was late, as usual, and we were waiting. My seat is next to Feona because we are both "H's." What made her do it, I don't know, but she got up and went to the front of the class and began impersonating Mrs. Caskey. Oh, she was very good. She walked like her and talked like her. Great entertainment! Mrs. Caskey has a way of putting her nose in the air and looking down on us with her glittering tiny eyes. She purses her lips and spits out the words. She is all business and no nonsense.

Feona began talking about the thyroid gland and all that can go wrong and how a malfunction can affect the entire body. She said, "Students, today we are continuing our study of the Endocrine System. The thyroid is a very important gland that controls and regulates much in the human body. Too much hormone produced by this gland can be detected by certain symptoms such as increased energy, loss of appetite and bulging eyes. This is called hyperthyroidism. Hypothyroidism is quite the opposite. Symptoms include thinning hair, tendency to gain weight and laziness. I do believe about one half of this class is suffering from the latter!"

By this time we were all howling. At the doorway, taking it all in, stood Mrs. Caskey. Feona was totally unaware of her presence but as each of us began to notice, the laughter trickled down to a few giggles here and there. Then Feona looked at the doorway, saw Mrs. Caskey and even for a red head, the blush was extraordinary. With a gasp, she rushed to her seat and waited for the hammer to fall.

Surprise!   Mrs. Caskey complimented her on her approach to teaching and with no change in her facial expression, said, "Well, Hartman, maybe you should consider going ahead for a degree and come back to fill in when I'm a little tardy." She then continued right on with the day's planned lecture. This little incident was apparently never reported to Mrs. Rivers. Feona didn't get a summons. Mrs. Caskey, we discovered was extremely kind. We were surprised but relieved. Not often were such actions discovered without dire consequences.

So many changes we have endured over the last year. I'm learning much, all I need to; but much more than any young lady should have to. Growing up in the country never prepared me for all that is involved in this "becoming a nurse" adventure. Medicine is a foreign world. I'm not sure if it is the life for me. Before, when I looked at nurses, I was impressed by their commitment to the sick and it all looked rather nice. Now I find all is not as appeared. Nurses work very hard and student training is intense and it is difficult to manage all the emotions; anxiousness, fear, anger, stress, plus sadness and grief. Survival with any self esteem at all intact is questionable. We are surrounded by constant criticism and fault finding. I would love to, but dropping out is not an option. Each day finished is closer to graduation and then I will decide whether I want to be a working nurse.

So how important is laughter? As necessary as breathing. That's why I love Feona. She dares to do all sort of crazy things. She makes me laugh; just hearing her laugh makes me laugh. "A merry heart is good medicine," it says so in the Bible. Medicine within medicine, the cure for most of my ills. God must have seen to it that I would be seated next to Feona.

Chapter 28
Room with a View
Jill

How can it still be two long hours to go? I started early this morning I haven't stopped running. Assigned four patients for a.m. cares at first and then they added a fifth. After delivering breakfast and lunch trays and feeding one patient each time, I have had enough. Mrs. Willis has used the bed pan five times. Room call lights are twinkling like stars. We need extra staff to meet the onslaught. Two nurse's aides called in sick today. I keep looking at the hall clock every time I travel up and down this irritating hall. "On the floor" must mean literally on the floor and crawling out the door when duty time is at last over.

Today I really want to get out of here because Reva and I are moving to our new room, second floor of the brand new Nurses' Home Wing. We have watched the progression towards completion for many months, convinced the project would never be finished. The construction workers put up brick walls at the end of the halls after they removed the stair wells and just last week they took those down and put up canvas between the old and the new. Some of us snuck over (not allowed) and explored the new rooms and they look so much bigger than our little cell. How nice it will be to have extra space.

The contractors who put up the brick walls apparently found a way to see through them. They drilled tiny holes in the mortar between the bricks and were watching us walk up and down the hall in various stages of undress. They were overheard at lunch at the hospital comparing notes. Our protectors put an end to that. The next day when we arrived up on our hall after classes, screens had been placed blocking their view. Imaging Peeking Toms right down the hall!

Finally it's time to leave the hospital, off duty at last. I rush over to my room. Reva is already packing up her stuff. It doesn't take me long to throw my meager possessions together and we are off to our new room. We hurried up and signed up for "ours" as soon as the list went up because we wanted one of the rooms that didn't face the hospital, but rather the side where we can look out at trees, bushes and lovely flowers.

Room 220 – a room with a view. It is wonderful! Two beds, both sitting on the floor (I can now sleep lower than two feet from the ceiling), two dressers with one large mirror, two desks with chairs, two bedside tables and two large closets. We can have more than three friends visit at one time without one standing in the hall. The window is at least six feet in width and right into our room is a scene that includes the outdoors

65

with a splendid panorama of trees and flowers. Reva said no matter how bad our day, we can come here and escape into the green forest and so we did that the very first day.

After unloading all our things we went to get a coke and Reva, who stopped earlier at the hospital lobby newsstand and bought two five cent candy bars, gave me one We had a toast and a great treat in celebration, flopped on our new beds, relaxed and enjoyed the moment.

One year completed and two to go and then freedom. We will be professionals with a R.N. behind our name if we can just endure another 24 months.

That evening we took showers in the new common bathroom. What a difference! There are six showers, eight sinks and six toilets. The toilets are in stalls that I can even turn around in, they seem to flush properly too. One very large bathtub sits in its own room. If I have time someday, I can actually sit in hot water and relax.

Our beds are so comfortable and we will sleep on mattresses not slept on before tonight. Remembering that the time there will be short (the alarm is set for 5:30 a.m.), I intend to enjoy every sleeping minute. Reva won't even insist that we house clean, the room is sparking clean.

We are going to put up the blind after "lights out" so we can see the stars. Isn't that a lovely thought?

Sweet dreams in new digs, a room with a view.

Chapter 29
The Royal Court
Jo Jo

My second year and I'm beginning to figure it all out, this Wayside Hospital business. There is quite a lot going on around here that isn't visible at first. As I see it, this place is just like a monarchy with its own King and Queen at the top. The Hospital Administrator, Mr. Morehouse, is the King, in charge of finance and the general running of things. The doctors are Lords or Earls. Mrs. Rivers (Queen Elizabeth I) is in charge of all the Ladies in Waiting, which includes nursing supervisors, head nurses, nursing instructors, clinical instructors, general staff nurses, aides, orderlies (men in white) and last and certainly least about one hundred student nurses (the peasants), all answerable to the Queen. Nothing goes unnoticed; the building is full of spies. There seems to be much jockeying for position, pushing aside and climbing up an invisible ladder to get closer to the Queen.

Each Med-Surg floor has a head nurse and each runs her own domain her unique way. I have been to all of them and as Mom always says, "Keep your eyes open and your mouth shut." I observed many interesting things, so noted:

4 North – Four four-patient wards, the rest double rooms, except for two private ones. This head nurse has her priorities in order. Everybody works. Even the patients seem to note this and calmness covers the place. Here students need their walking shoes.

3 North – All private rooms with private bathrooms. The wealthy and influential are admitted here. The head nurse bows and scrapes to the sick guests. Everything is very clean, much scrubbing and dusting is going on. There are always plenty of clean, crisp linens and the food trays from dietary are delivered here first (so hot foods will be hot and cold will be cold). The students must also bow and scrape and carry around a dust cloth.

2 North – Four, six to seven patient wards with the rest double rooms, two common bathrooms, one male and one female, beds for the blue collar class. The head nurse here is a little dippy. She is obsessed with supplies and she hangs on to them for dear life. (I heard there is a bonus each year to the head nurse who keeps costs down). Don't ever break a thermometer on this unit or need a band aide. Bribes are needed for clean sheets, getting an extra pillow is impossible. The assignments given to students are on over load and extremely difficult to complete. The staff nurses and aides take lots of breaks for coffee and cigarettes. Patient's lights must be answered by, of course, you-know-who. A student needs skates here.

2 South – Four, six to seven patient wards, one four patient ward, the rest double rooms and two single rooms (no bathrooms) for terminally ill or very noisy patients, two common bathrooms, one for each sex. Census is highest of all units, usually fifty or above if the cubbie holes in the hall are used. Mostly the very poor and welfare patients are admitted here. The Head Nurse needs all her stamina just to keep her head above water, but somehow finds time to help move a patient, make beds and assist in giving out the food trays. The work load here is endless and exhausting, the hall is so long, so many patients, so many needs. By far the most difficult of all the floors to work on. Somehow, though, it's my favorite. We are a team pulling together. A student needs her running shoes, but everyone is running.

I'm curious about the specialties and how these areas are run. I've yet to enter my first one. However, I do have a little idea how it will be for me in surgery. Working 3 North I was told to take some catherization trays to the surgical supply room inside the surgery unit. Walking through the door, I saw a nurse standing in the hallway. "Hey you," I said "Can you please tell me where the supply room is?" She looked at me rather scornfully and said, "It is on your left at the end of the hall and my name is not 'Hey You', in fact, it's Mrs. Farley. Your name please?" I meekly told her my name. She informed me, "I will be waiting for you when you come to surgery. I am Head Nurse here and will be anxious to teach you some manners and the proper way to address your superiors."

Should I bury myself alive?

"Please, Blessed Mother, let her forget what happened this day. Surgery for me is just two weeks away."

All in all, no matter how important the big wigs think they are, King and Queen included, the only reason Wayside Hospital exists is because of the patients who come here. No patients and the doors will close. This place is dependent upon the sick and miserable among us. The only really happy area might be with the newborns, but even suffering proceeds that joy. Giving my best only helps a little, but I hope I will always remember – patients are always first, that is the only real reason for wearing the uniform. The King and Queen are not number one, after all.

Chapter 30
OB, Oh Boy
Rachel

Obstetrics Specialty, I have been here now four weeks. The time spent is divided up in several different areas. My first two weeks I was assigned to labor and delivery. Katie and I were there together. Mrs. Williamson was the head nurse and we already had several classes with her about the unit. She looked quite elderly, at least fifty five years old, a bit grumpy, and never smiled. What's with these old nurses who look so mean? We started the first day sitting with two mothers-to-be who were in fairly active labor, Katie in one room and me in the other. We first prepared them for delivery with a prep (shave) using a very dull razor (where do they buy these things?). After shaving, we were told to pour antiseptic liquid over the area. There was lots of wiggling, squealing about the burning, but it pales in comparison to what lies ahead. Also an enema was given to clear the lower colon and then we were to sit beside her, time her pains (contractions), take vital signs, plus check and record fetal heart beats. One of the RNs came in now and then to do an exam and check cervical dilatation. When delivery became eminent, the patient was transferred to the delivery room where the real fun begins.

I know women have babies but I had no idea how terribly unpleasant the process. The student nurse (me) assists the doctor, handing sponges, instruments, medications, sutures, etc. We, of course, are all dressed up in gowns, masks and sterile gloves. What a messy business, all sorts of fluids are flying around and there is much moaning and some screaming. Finally the little one is born, the cord is cut and everyone collectively holds their breath until the little baby takes a breath. The first time I was so thrilled, the baby was so little but looking around with blinking bright eyes, as if to say, "What am I doing here?" What a miracle! The mother is now quiet and usually smiling. How brave they are!

After mother and child are whisked away to their rooms, the cleaning up begins. Guess who does that? Our instructor barks, "The laundry doesn't appreciate any sheets with blood clots on them so be careful and remove them all." Nobody told me this was part of the picture. Picking blood clots off sheets while the rest of the staff is laughing, drinking coffee and smoking in the break room. The world is not a nice place. After doing this about five times, I hated hearing, "We are going to have a baby so get scrubbed up." All in all, I scrubbed for forty-two deliveries in two weeks. Katie had forty. One of us was on call every evening beginning at 4 p.m. until 7 a.m. the next morning and all day Saturday and Sundays. At night we slept in an empty room on the ward, and no matter how many times we were up at night, work and classes loomed ahead the next day. The nurses keep harping about a "full moon", whatever that means. Anyhow, I think those two weeks set a record for births. Couldn't they stop some of these ladies at the front door and send them to the other hospital in town? Total exhaustion couldn't even describe our state. We would gladly give two years of our lives for eight hours of uninterrupted sleep. After our last day in labor and delivery, Katie and I celebrated with long hot showers and dropping into our beds. At last we were finished with the baby-birthing ordeal. Two more students were assigned. Delivery has an endless supply of slave labor.

Next week we were in new-born nursery. What a difference! I love looking at their little wrinkled faces and the response of relatives at the nursery viewing windows. Most of all, I love carrying the babies to their mothers. Could these ladies be the same ones that were screaming in the delivery room? They smile, coo and kiss the little ones, apparently pushing that ghastly experience behind them. A happy ending and even I am beginning to forget what it took to get to this result. Happy mother and family! Seldom seen at other units at Wayside.

Of course there are always exceptions. Two weeks later I was out on the floor taking care of a new mother. Rumor was around that yesterday there was a stillbirth. Today I discovered it was true and the mother is my patient. The staff was very kind putting her into a private room away from the newborn nursery. It was difficult to go into her room. How to handle this one? No one has given me counsel. She smiled at me as I entered through the door. She is so young, pretty and seems so sweet. We began to talk about general things, the weather and so on. Then one of the nursery nurses came in holding a baby. She stopped and said "Oh, I'm so sorry. I have the wrong room" and quickly exited. Tears coursed down my patient's cheeks and I stood there unable to speak. How devastating it must feel to have such high hopes coming in here and then to leave with empty arms? So against all that impersonal stiff upper lip stuff, I just hugged her and we cried together; a time that would break hearts and haunt dreams. Could it be that nursing isn't just about giving a.m. cares, emptying bed pans, and rolling people around in beds? Maybe a lot of it is being there when needed. I think even I can do that. Going through all that crazy stuff, doing all the grunt work like cleaning up after childbirth puts me in that place. If I hadn't been there, I wouldn't be much good here.

Chapter 31
The Scream
Feona

Seven of us are sitting around in Reva and Jill's room moaning about our terrible day. Pauline is complaining about her a.m., care duties. It seemed she had just finished the whole complete deal with a Mrs. Scott whose body was one-half paralyzed due to a stroke. Proud that she had managed it all by herself, she was about to leave the room when a loud, gurgling sound came from the bed and sure enough, Mrs. Scott had just had the largest liquid bowel movement Pauline had ever seen and she had to repeat the whole process again. She thought about pretending she wasn't there for the big blow out but didn't have the heart to leave Mrs. Scott in such a mess. Guess what? Fifteen minutes late for class and Mrs. Caskey wasn't a bit happy.

Jo Jo had to scrub for "Old Red Top" and he was in one of his terrible moods, as always; cursing and throwing things around, treating everyone foul, especially Jo Jo. Everyone in the operating room was dancing around to his tune and she couldn't understand it. How did the doctors get away with such obnoxious behavior?

Reva spent the entire morning doing treatments on 2 North which included, three enemas, two douches (what's with all the douches?), seven urine tests for diabetic patients, several wound dressings, two sterile perineal cares (I won't even try to explain that one) and learning how to change a colostomy bag. All those procedures have something to do with lower body functions, except for the wound dressings. All rather offensive for sure!

I was medicine girl for 2 South and had two every hour milk and creams for patients with stomach ulcers, each at the opposite ends of the long hall. I almost swallowed a few myself just to save another run down the hall, but I never could stand milk and I would surely vomit. By the time I went off duty my feet were crying out for a good soak.

Jill was the only one who had a short duty day. She fainted when one of her patients started to spit up blood and she was sent over to the nurses' home. What is going on with that girl? She keeps passing out!

Reva said she was told one time, if tensions are high and nerves rattled, that a good loud scream would really help. We ask her to demonstrate, so she opened the window and let out a piercing scream that filled the air. "So there," she said, "I feel much better." Hooting laugher, we all agreed with her, just <u>hearing</u> someone scream seemed to help.

About ten minutes later the darkness around our nursing home was lit up with flashing red lights and sirens were wailing. We watched from the window as policemen began searching the grounds with flashlights. What was happening? Girls were running down the hall saying that they think someone was attacked and raped. A terrible scream was heard coming from near the nurses' home over at the hospital and the police were called. Just think, one of our very own raped and maybe even murdered!

Believe me, we weren't admitting to anything, we didn't even hear a scream. How could we possibly explain Reva's actions to anyone? She was already in big trouble because she and Jill left a coke bottle in their room and hung their crinolines on the window blind to dry, forgetting to remove them before room inspection. They both received four demerits and they are three away from being "campused."

I must say, the firemen and policemen did a diligent search. They didn't give up for at least an hour of tramping all over the place looking for a victim. They asked Mrs. Stone our housemother, if anyone inside heard anything. Some heard "but had no idea where the scream came from." It seemed they were quite disappointed to find nothing.

Quite an exciting evening and we were certainly distracted from all the woes of that day. Reva was right, "A good loud scream relieves tensions," in very unexpected ways. After that incident we decided, if necessary, we would scream in a closet. It might not produce the same results but the risk was too great for a repeat performance. People around here didn't go in for false alarms.

Chapter 32
Caring for the Little Ones
Pauline

Pediatrics – anything and everything one needs to know about children. Our classes were extensive. Normal Growth and Development had to be first studied so we would recognize all that can happen to children that is a danger to normal growth and development. Apparently great strides have been made in the last hundred years. In the last century the mortality rate was very high. Now vaccines have been developed that have greatly decreased the infectious diseases that had been so devastating. Of course there are other dangers lurking, injuries due to falls, burns, ingestion of caustic poisonous substances, birth defects, treatment and prevention, and on and on it goes. Some of the classes were interesting but most were drop dead boring. Believe it or not, I did manage to pass the numerous tests and now here I am heading to the Pediatric Unit for "practical experience", forgetting most of the stuff that was poured into my head.

Walking through the doors was like entering a whole new world. In ten rooms there were 43 children (full capacity), from newborns (born before getting to Wayside in time and not allowed in the Newborn Nursery) to twelve and thirteen year olds. The toddlers were in rooms in cribs with nets over them to prevent falls, most were wailing. Some were in croup tents and others in oxygen tents. High chairs were lined up along the walls and the nurses' station was a little cubbie hole with a long desk on one side and medicines were stored in cupboards on the other wall. On down the hall were rooms filled with older children. The boy's ward was in an uproar. One boy was jumping off the end of his bed hanging on to his robe sash, like a real-life Tarzan. The other boys were cheering him on, including one with one leg incased in a cast from thigh to ankle and the leg had a weight hanging from the end of his foot. He looked like he would love to join Tarzan and try to add another broken leg so he would have a matched pair. Some of the older kids were running in and out of their rooms and the nurses were shouting at them to get back in their beds.

Phones were ringing and carts were traveling up and down the hall carrying children to x-ray and surgery. What a place! Chaos! Chaos!

After one week in this place I thought a nervous breakdown was just around the corner. Try giving liquid medicine to a spitting toddler. I was covered with sticky stuff. I had more on me than ever got to their stomachs. Shots were very difficult. You needed two nurses, one to hold the wiggler down and one to give the injection and the kids weren't fooled. When two of us walked in to their room and headed to their bed the battle began, they had seen this before! We fed and rocked, gave breathing treatments, (that included pulling the portable oxygen tank to the bedside) changed dressings, changed diapers, changed sheets and gowns frequently. We were in the changing business. At shifts end I looked like I had been to war.

But somehow, and I can't explain it, I began to love it. I suppose I had become rather tired of adult patients. Many were so demanding and difficult. They acted like I was their own private slave nurse and didn't have anything else to do but cater to their every wish. Not so with kids, satisfied with very little, they are easy to please. Holding the little ones and giving them comfort was special. I felt for once in this whole student nursing experience I was making a difference. Not noted by anyone but those in my arms.

Little Scotty was six months old, a sweet little fellow his diagnosis on admission was pneumonia, both lungs. He was poorly dressed, very thin and apparently hadn't been bathed in a while. After bathing him I carried him into his room. Having a little time, I held him and rocked him while the oxygen tent was made ready. It was touch and go those first few days, then we began to see remarkable changes. Breathing easier and with x-ray evidence, the oxygen was discontinued. His appetite improved and he became all bright and perky. We began to know each other and he would reach out his arms to me when I walked in his room.

After three weeks, Scotty was ready for discharge. The doctor told the head nurse to notify the parents, who, by the way, had never visited, nor could anyone recall a phone call. The parents could not be found. They had moved from the area with no forwarding address. Little Scotty had been abandoned. How could any mother move away leaving her little baby behind? I couldn't even comprehend this. My mother always told everyone she would "climb to the moon" for me. My mind couldn't take in desertion. The next day a social worker came and took Scotty. He was going into foster care. Tears flowed. He would never remember how we all cheered him on through those scary, very sick days, but I knew I would never ever forget him.

Some very amusing incidents happened. One day the desk phone rang and one of the roving boys who had escaped from his room answered. I quickly grabbed the phone and who was on the other end but "Old Red Hood" and he shouted, "So the kids are answering the phone now. Where are all the nurses, at lunch?" I tried to explain, but he would have none of it. He cursed and fumed. Finally after the tirade was over he settled down and gave me an order which I couldn't accept because I was a student. I caught one of the graduate nurses and gave her the phone, loud squawking noises came from the phone. She became very pale and looked at me with daggers in her eyes. Not my fault! I don't make the rules!

Later that day when Grace and I were in our room, we had a good laugh, a graduate nurse in trouble. Once in a great while things even up just a little.

The weeks flew by and my last day came. I didn't want to leave. Nursing would be great if I could stay with the kids. I decided if I get through everything ahead and actually finish, I will be a Pediatric Nurse. Now my goal is set! So onward and upward we go over the humps and bumps ahead. Now I know where I belong and someday I may walk into chaos, chaos, chaos, loving it!

Chapter 33
A Tempest over a Teapot Lid
Reva

The daily drag on the Med-Surg floors was beginning to get to me. We were always racing at top speed, trying to make it to the 11 a.m. finish line so we could have lunch and not be late for those never ending afternoon classes.

Checking the schedule on the bulletin board, I discovered that low and behold, next Monday I was to report to Diet Kitchen at 4:30 a.m. What a nice change. Fixing up trays of food for patients rather than emptying their bedpans. Things should be more pleasant for once not having to deal with what exits the other end of the digestive system.

The Dietician, Mrs. Surry, has been teaching classes on Nutrition and Diet Therapy. She is a tiny little lady, looks like she has never had a proper meal in her whole life. It is a sure thing, no doubt, that she never eats bread (my mother bakes the best) and frowns at the very thought of cake, pie, cookies or candy. In class she continually speaks of lettuce, spinach, broccoli and chick peas. I could care less where the body stores Vitamin A, how iron builds blood and all that calorie counting is for the birds. We don't have to stress out about that as all our meals are prepared for us. We eat whatever we can get our hands on and we are not about to turn down a cookie. Many calories are needed to keep up the maddening pace. I haven't gained one extra pound since I came into this crazy place.

The first day in Diet Kitchen was indeed an eye-opener. After setting up the special diet breakfast trays and sending them off to the floors, we had to prepare mid-morning snacks, which were delivered by me to special diet patients all over the hospital. Next were the lunch trays followed by the preparation of mid-afternoon snacks before heading off to class. You are kidding, non-stop running around. My legs are aching and my feet are killing me. Didn't this whole hospital have one place where a student could catch a breath?

Mrs. Surry is always bossing me around and her assistant, Miss Coat, is a real pain. She drank coffee and rested while I took off with the mid-mornings.

One morning as I was preparing breakfast trays, Miss Coat was actually helping. I was placing the little ceramic tea pots on the trays and we ran out of tops. Miss Coat informed me that all the teapots going to 3 North (the floor for the higher-ups) must have tops. If there were not enough tops, 2 South could go without. Well, it was definitely a mistake but

I put my foot down and told her that when I ran out of tops, 2 South would get them and the big wigs could go without for once.

You would have thought I dropped the atomic bomb. "How dare I speak to her with such disrespect? Who did I think I was? Student nurses do not refuse to do what their supervisors command!" From that moment on, it was war and for the rest of my days there, life was Hell (sorry mom). Miss Coat had me even mopping the floors. Not all bad, patients on 2 South got their tea pot lids.

At the end of each stay in anyplace, we were all given an evaluation which we must read and sign. Mine was not very good (a big surprise). Apparently, Miss Coat complained to Mrs. Surry about me. She reported "I didn't follow orders well, I was not efficient with my time, I was sometimes late giving out snacks," and so on. I could refuse to sign but why put another fagot on the fire? A trip to Mrs. Rivers' office first followed by a letter home, was the procedure for uncooperative students. All terribly unfair but very little about this place is fair. So sign it I did, I even handed it back with a smile.

However, Jill told me something very informative about Miss Coat. One day, while working on "the big wig floor," she darted into a room where Dr. Davis was a patient and Miss Coat was in a very compromising position with certain said married doctor. Aha! Caught red faced and guilty. Miss Coat knows that Jill and I are roommates and every time I see her I give her a knowing look. The enemy has been flanked. There is a God after all!

Chapter 34
Isolation - All by Myself
Grace

At the end of the Pediatric Unit is another unit called the Isolation Ward. Here all ages with communicable diseases and infections are placed. There are eight private rooms with baths and an in-room sink for washing hands by staff and visitors.

We have been taught isolation procedures which involves wearing of gowns, gloves and masks as needed, depending on the patient's illness. Food trays are not allowed in the rooms but food must be carried in on paper plates, liquids in paper cups and plastic utensils for eating. Each time we enter a room we must dress up as warranted. Before leaving the room we must remove all this extra stuff and place in special marked laundry bags. All trash is emptied following each shift and placed in special containers. It is triple, triple, triple the work done on other wards and believe it or not, we work by ourselves. No aides, no one to answer the phone. When a patient is called to x-ray, back up can be had from "Peds." Everyone hates working in isolation.

Now it is my turn. Almost every time I'm all gowned up and in a room with a patient the phone rings. So it is; undress, wash hands, leave the room and run to the phone. Then dress back up and return to the room. The lady in Room Three has a boil on her arm that has to have 15 minute warm wet compresses every three hours and Room five has a nine year old with measles and has breathing treatments scheduled for 20 minutes every four hours. How do I handle all this? There is only one empty room, so there are seven other patients to look after plus giving out all the meds. By the end of this shift they will have to cart me off. Why is it when a graduate nurse works here she almost always has an aide?

After two days my hands are red and raw, my feet are hurting and I can't keep my hair neat under those dreadful things we have to wear on our heads. Why do I even bother with those bobby pins every night?

Interesting that when a doctor comes to isolation to see his patients, a "Peds" nurse will show up to make rounds with him. Wouldn't you know it? What is it about these men that nurses fawn around them so? Few are nice, and not only that, fewer still are good looking and none are bachelors. There are rumors flying around that one senior student is sneaking around with one of the doctors, playing with fire for sure. One thing a senior must have is more free time. Last month I went on a date with a guy I knew from high school and fell asleep in the movie. Embarrassing! He told me he would see me again sometime. Romance is off the radar for now.

I'm rushing around trying to finish up (no classes today). I know there isn't a hope of being done on time, but Pauline is here. She had a little down time in "Peds" so she came to help. Bless her heart, she is finishing up all those crazy chores, emptying trash cans, relining them, putting out gowns and masks for the next shift and so forth. I can give out the 2 p.m. meds, finish charting and get the report written for the 3-11 nurse. Without Pauline this would not be possible. The next shift nurse is never happy if the previous nurse is not ready to turn the unit over to her.

Done for the day, only two more days and my time here will be over at last. No more working in isolation, Hip, Hip, Hooray. Little did I know then that a rash of polio patients would come in the next summer and I would be here again.

Tonight I'm getting into that new tub for a long hot soak. I may even skip dinner. Maybe I can get mom to bring some food. Home cooked food, so much better than anything you can find at the Wayside Cafeteria, its worth two demerits if caught. I will gladly share my "from home meal" with dear Pauline.

Chapter 35
Creative Recreation
Katie

The class of 1959 (that's us) now touts the name the party class. Several students got together and decided there needed to be life after work and classes. In the beginning of our second year, they requested permission to have a few parties to celebrate the holidays. The recreation-classroom has a stereo player with records we can play and many go down there sometimes during our free time, relax and catch our breath after exhausting days. This is where we will have our parties. Given permission we all agreed on Halloween, Christmas, Valentine's Day and St. Patrick's Day. We will plan the parties and invite the other classes to join.

Halloween – we pooled our meager resources, bought apples to bob for (water in a barrel), Halloween cupcakes, and candy. Lindsay brought some pumpkins from her grandmother's garden and we carved some mean looking jack-o-lanterns. Our costumes were made up of anything we could find and scrape together. Some wore their poodle skirts, put their hair up in pony tails and wore saddle shoes. One tiny girl (a senior) wore a diaper (made out of a towel) and a tee shirt. Reva and Jill blacked their faces and came as Uncle Tom and Little Liza. I covered myself with a sheet with holes for eyes (not very original). Feona led us in some silly songs and we danced to records and told ghost stories. All in all, we had a great time.

Christmas – We cut out snowflakes and gathered greens from the evergreens on the grounds, wrapped up some funky presents, Band-Aides, gauze sponges, old rubber gloves, anything we could find that was loose and wouldn't be missed. Some girls baked cookies and decorated them. We whipped up a refreshing punch (no alcohol, of course, the house mothers were checking it out). Rachel played the piano and we all sang Christmas carols and several of the girls did a Jingle Bell dance. We drew numbers for the gifts. Mine was an old bed pan to use as a sled. It works great!

Valentine's Day – Homemade paper Valentine hearts were strung around the room on string with pink and red streamers hanging about. Reva decorated a box for Valentine cards. Jo Jo bought a large bag of signature candy hearts which we all read to one another. We invited the doctors we liked and a few actually stopped by for a while and shared with us cookies, candy and punch (red this time). Boyfriends were invited and showed up (no one could leave the room with one). The house mothers were watching us like hawks. No PDA (Public Display of Affection) was allowed, Valentine's Day without any kisses, old fogies they are. Mrs. Strong is always telling us we must save ourselves for marriage. No young man wants his candy previously unwrapped.

St. Patrick's Day – It was time for a little variety, so we planned a spaghetti dinner with green spaghetti (dyed with green food coloring) and green punch. The punch thing was getting a little old so we added after dinner coffee and tea. If any of us had anything green, we wore it. For entertainment two girls sang some Irish tunes. Ouch! Some others did a Can, Can Dance. Their kicks were off but we cheered them on anyhow. Were they really wearing green panties? Laughter bounced off the walls. The house mothers even smiled a little.

Other recreation opportunities – the city provides us with free passes to the community swimming pool in the summer and the YMCA indoor pool in the winter, a treat for sure on hot summer days and boring winter ones.

We walk and walk all over town on nice warm sunny days and new snow days. We walk down to the huge railway station (built in 1850) to watch the passengers get on and off the trains. We go to the Creamery and buy ice cream – three scoops for five cents. If we have a quarter we go to one of the three downtown movie theaters and swoon over the male movie stars and wonder what it might be like to be a star like glamorous Ava Gardner or beautiful Elizabeth Taylor. We discover little openings under the trees at the park near the nursing home and have picnics with sandwiches left over from p.m. snacks the night before. And oh yes, we do go out on dates. Most of us are boy crazy, dreaming of the day we will find the right one and fall madly in love, get married and live happily ever after like in fairy tales or in the movies.

Some go to the dance halls on Friday and Saturday nights. Most of all, we love going home. Seeing our families reminds us that a normal life is still out there. One of the worst things is to be stuck at the nurses' home mostly alone for the entire weekend.

Cloistered like nuns, breakouts are as vital as breathing. If fun can be found we will find it. When I look back I am struck by how innocent we all were about life's realities, but we are learning quickly how sad it can all be. We try to maintain some kind of balance with all types of diversions.

We now are masters of laughter and instigators of all sorts of crazy schemes. We push each other in laundry carts up and down our hallway. We ran around on the flat roof of the new addition the other night. Apparently we were seen by someone over at the hospital and a notice was sent over, "No one is allowed on the roof." The next time we go up we will keep our heads down.

We once arranged a tennis match with four of the doctors who played doubles while we all shouted and cheered. We made up silly songs about hospital duty to popular tunes of the day and willingly share with each other our daily experiences, amusing stores and collective complains as to how we are being misused and abused.

Yes, we are the party girls, hunger for laughter. Our spirits are lifted by making our down time an escape from all that worries us. Each of us finds ways to forget and endure. Some attend Bible study and prayer meetings. Visiting our home churches and all the friends there is part of our weekends away for most of us.

Being together, facing the same challenges, enjoying good times and bad times is creating in us a lasting sisterhood. Creative-recreation is a necessary necessity for young ladies in our extraordinary circumstances.

Chapter 36
Terminal
Rachel

Looking at my assignment for the morning, I couldn't stop the sinking feeling in my stomach. This is the third morning straight I will have Mrs. Dudley for "a.m." care. The poor lady is dying from cancer and is in the final stages. It is so difficult walking into her room because no matter how hard I try or what I do, I can't make her comfortable, but the worst part of it all is the continuing lie. Radical surgery, if possible is the only treatment for a person who receives this terrible diagnosis. Some experimental treatments such as radiation implants are being tried, but the only hope for most is the post surgery remark, "We think we got it all." Well, apparently Mrs. Dudley was told that and no they didn't "get it all." Now here she is terminal and close to the end. Her family doesn't want her to know and so we are dancing around the truth. Yesterday, she asked me straight out and I stammered a few words saying "Well, you need to talk to your doctor about your concerns." She went on to tell me how she didn't understand why she was feeling so bad and in such terrible pain if indeed the cancer was gone. I had been cautioned by the staff to be very careful when talking to Mrs. Dudley, "Don't let her know the diagnosis. Her family will be very upset."

Why would they do this to her? Surely she will be able to figure it out and she will hate us all for deceiving her so. No one has taught me how to deal with such a dilemma, it is surely someone else's turn to have her for "a.m." cares.

Last evening some of my student nursing friends were talking about the number of cancer patients on the wards. All in all they counted twenty five patients in Wayside in some stage of the disease. Some are heading home, hoping for the best, most will return and not a few will die here. Most families can't deal with watching their loved ones in the final hours. So they die in a strange place around strangers with family members popping in and out of their rooms. We could see the need to have nurses trained specifically to help the poor patients and their loved ones weather such dark times.

But right now, I'm on my own with Mrs. Dudley. It seems the most difficult patients are given to students because the graduate nurses don't want to handle such trying circumstances if someone else is available. We are easy scapegoats for sure.

Oh dear, she is really under it today, half asleep, but I have to get on with "a.m." cares and be off the floor by 11:30 a.m. at the latest. She must have been medicated just awhile ago. "Mrs. Dudley time for your bath," I called out. Struggling awake she manages a smile and tells me how glad she is to see me and how nice it is to have the same nurse. Stating, "There are so many different ones. I'm hoping to go home in a few days. I know I could get well quicker if I were on my own turf, so to speak. I get so homesick here."

I have never before felt so sad, but I must not show it – it's called "putting on a happy face." Getting through the bath and bed change took quite a while. Finally I finished and was getting ready to go on to the next patient when Mrs. Dudley said, "Miss Lucas, you know what I truly think? I think no one is telling me the truth, I don't even want to admit it to myself but I believe I am dying and I can understand why everyone is pretending. They don't want me to give up hope. So really, it's okay, don't worry about your part in this. I know all about following orders. I was a student nurse myself for two years and I quit. I couldn't handle it. Hospital work was not my calling for sure. But you, you have what it takes so stick with it. When you walk in my room, somehow no matter how I feel, it seems the sun starts shining."

What could I say? To think I didn't want my "a.m." cares to include Mrs. Dudley. I thanked her for her encouraging words and I'm sorry, but I couldn't stop the tears. I feel so utterly selfish. Instead of thinking how I could make her day better, I was thinking only of myself and my terrible assignment. She opened my eyes to seeing the patient, not as some job that needed to be done, but as a service of caring to even the most hopeless cases.

So I hope my tomorrow's assignment will be the same as today's.

I'm not the same person who walked in Wayside doors a little over a year ago with a rosy attitude about life. I'm changing and growing every day hopefully for the better. This "hands on" nursing is really the best teacher. Many thanks to patients like Mrs. Dudley, maybe one day I'll deserve to wear my cap with the black stripe added. A diploma graduate RN!

Chapter 37
Anticipating Needs
Lindsay

One year, eight months, two days have gone by since I came to this place and almost nothing is as anticipated. So far I have been on every Med-Surg floor except this one, 3 North, I began here a week ago, the floor with the supposed easiest assignments. There are fewer patients but most have a "you are my servant attitude." They probably have maids at home. Some, however, are very kind and only put their call light on when they truly need attention.

"Anticipating the patient's needs" seems to be the necessary factor that makes one a "good" nurse. When I started this whole deal I had no idea what that meant, but the light is coming on. I can now recognize pain by facial features and groans. Sometimes patients look just uncomfortable and the clinical instructors have taught me how to position and place pillows to help. We need to prevent complications by preventative measures, such as, make sure bowels are moving, watch out for pressure sores, pay close attention to vital signs, chills and fevers, assess breathing problems, abdominal pain, wound drainage, urine output and the list goes on and on. I've discovered it takes months of classes and many, many hours of working to even come close to being on top of it all.

This morning I have five patients assigned to me. Thankfully all are at the same end of the hall. Instead of one medicine girl for the entire ward they are trying out a new system called "total care." Because of this I also have to give medications to my assigned patients. I need my skates. Mrs. Lake is recovering from abdominal surgery (this morning will be her first time out of bed). Mrs. Saunders had a heart attack and is on complete bed rest, Mrs. Owen's diagnosis is unknown (complains of terrible back pain). Mrs. Morgan had cataract surgery (she has to lie flat, her head flanked by two sand bags) and Dr. Fungi has pneumonia and will have to have a penicillin injection at 10 a.m. (oh no!) That is four complete bed baths and pans of hot water for Dr. Fungi, the only one who can actually move around and bathe himself.

Moving along without too much trouble it's now 9:45 a.m, I have two patients completed and now it is time for Dr. Fungi's shot. My knees are weak as I head to his room with a filled syringe on a little tray. This is a time when a girl really needs her mother. Could anyone feel more inadequate? What if I have trouble getting the needle in and cause pain?

Even worse, what if I miss the right upper quadrant and he is paralyzed for life? If I just had someone else's name on my sleeve instead of mine.

He is lying there reading a newspaper and I tell him I'm here to give him an injection. He looks at me with those blue eyes and says "What side would you have me turn to Miss Hinkle?" I stuttered out, "Left." He turned as instructed, lifted the sheet and waited. I measured (making an invisible x), wiped the area with an alcohol sponge and with trembling hands stuck the needle in as far as possible, aspirated and pushed in the plunger. He didn't yell – a good sign. I covered him back up quickly. One doesn't hesitate when a doctor's buttocks are exposed.

"Well, Miss Hinkle," he said, "I believe you have done that before. You could do with a little more practice, however that was a fair job. You looked like you might faint when you walked in here. It wasn't that much trouble, was it?" Now the baby blues are actually twinkling. Then he smiled at me – he really did! He is so handsome! I whispered "thank you" and almost ran from the room. My heart was pounding. I believe I might like to marry him. Not possible, he is already with wife number two according to rumors swirling around Wayside. In "anticipating the patient's needs" I guess he just needs clean sheets.

Chapter 38
A Month in the Sun
Reva

It's May of our second year and my schedule is confirmed. June will be my month off then beginning in July I will be going across state for three months at one of the state's Mental Hospitals, Summer Meadows, for what the higher ups call our Psychiatric Affiliation. I will not be back at Wayside until October. Going home is what most girls will be doing on their summer vacation, but I think it would be a great time to do something different. Wouldn't it be wonderful to spend a month in the sun at the beach? Jill can't go because her month off is August. Feona has the same schedule as I, so I am going to approach her with my plan.

Feona said, "Sure, and why not?" So we are full steam ahead with plans bouncing around in our heads. The first challenge is how to get there? I looked at different bus lines and their schedules. We can travel the 225 miles on a High Ways Bus, so this is the way to go – slow but cheap. Leaving the first Saturday in June, we were seated on the bus at 5 a.m. heading out for our summer beach adventure.

The second challenge is funds. After paying our bus fare the total amount between us was twenty dollars. We will have to find a job and right away. That should not be a problem. Summer resorts always need temporary help. With an eight hour a day job we should still have plenty of time on the beach.

The bus ride turned out to be exhausting and our packages of crackers and apples did little to stave off hunger. After ten hours of going down county roads, stopping at every train crossing and picking up passengers who were going ten miles then dropping them off, we reached the Jersey shore.

Oh, the ocean, beautiful blue with bright blue skies hovering above and lovely white caps hitting the shore, we were enthralled. This is the first time I had ever been to the ocean. However, we couldn't linger. Carrying our suitcases filled with our meager possessions, the first "must do" is to find a place to lie down our weary heads. The second hotel we went to offered us a room at the very top – more like a dorm, a long room with about twelve cot-like beds, no windows and one sink with only cold running water. A dollar a day – very cheap, so of course we took it. After a few hot dogs at a boardwalk stand we returned to the hotel, took showers at the common bathroom, one floor down, fell into our beds (sheets provided) and slept like the dead.

The next morning we were out on the boardwalk looking for a job. All the businesses unfortunately had already hired their summer help. We will be on the next bus back if we can't find something. Someone then told us about a diner out on one of the old beach roads that needed waitresses. So off we went and sure enough, we can work there, the place is named "The Gotta Eat Diner." They are open 24 hours a day, serving the early fisherman breakfast and then drop-ins the rest of the day.

Feona will be working 8 a.m. to 4 p.m. and I will be working nights 12 a.m. to 8 a.m. We will be passing each other coming and going. That is another problem. How would we come and go? Believe it or not, the owners offered to provide transportation to and from. Job found!

The diner looks like an abandoned railway car, very dreary with some neon lights draped around it. It should be named more correctly "The Dumpy Diner." Inside is even worse. Even the pictures on the walls are grease smeared. Oh for many buckets of hot water and bottles of strong disinfectant cleaner. There is a row of bar stools at the counter and booths around the walls. All need a fresh coat of paint. However, I wasn't hired for my decorating skills, I just need to make a little money so I can have fun in the sun. I can do something about keeping the tables and counters wiped and the dishes and eating utensils clean. Our salary is 35 cents an hour, plus tips.

Feona began work the next morning. I tried sleeping in but wasn't very successful. It is so hot! Arriving at our room late that afternoon, Feona gave me the low down on working for Mike, the owner. She was busy most of the morning pouring coffee and serving eggs in various forms and all those customers, mostly men, loved their ham and bacon. For lunch it was hamburgers and fries - the big sellers, plus sandwiches and soups. Some tips were collected and she returned that day with $8.58. Oh, and one other perk, we can eat our meals there for free. Mike won't allow any foul language around us and if anyone gets fresh he promises to throw them out. After all we are nursing students and if he had any daughters they would be about our age.

Since midnight is my starting time, Feona and I grabbed our swim suits and headed for the beach. What were we thinking? Both red heads who never turn brown, we quickly began to get red and dramatically increased our freckle count. Never being in the ocean before, we only ventured up to our knees. The waves hit the shore with amazing force and frequency and whacked us around pretty good. Wet sand coated us, but who cares? Lovely it is to be away from all those boring hospital duties and endless classes. We felt like free spirits, even though Feona suffered a rather severe sunburn and couldn't tolerate any amount of sun for the next week.

Midnight and I am on the job. This is the beer crowd and a jolly bunch they are and getting jollier by the minute. They stagger in and out of the diner shouting and singing. Amazing! I am completely out of my element.

Ike, who works all night, looks out for me. Mike, his brother, gave him a heads up about us. No funny business allowed. They became our protectors. About 4 a.m. the fishermen began to arrive and the coffee pots were emptied at a brisk rate and like Feona, I delivered the eggs. When 8 a.m. came Mike took me back to my hotel, I hit the bed just as Mike drove off with Feona. My take for my shift was $9.15. We are getting rich!

Exhausted after each of our shifts, we spent most of the time sleeping in the air-less room without air conditioning. Extremely hot! It is worse for me trying to sleep during the day time with my stomach digesting a greasy breakfast. I don't think after a week I could look at another egg, fried, scrambled, boiled or whatever. Speaking for myself I am switching to dry cereal.

The days are flying by and we see less and less of the ocean. If we are having fun it isn't in the sun.

What characters we are meeting. I like the feisty old fisherman best. Tanned and wrinkled, they are full of stories of their days out on the sea. It is a hard life but they have no bosses out there with only the water, birds and fish for company. Sounds heavenly.

Feona and I had stories to share too. They like to hear about living in the mountains and all things medical. Laughter rang out in the "Gotta Eat Diner." All in all, it was a good time and when the month was almost up we didn't want to leave. Mike and Ike told us they hated to see the two red heads go. We added flavor to the place. They couldn't remember a time when work was so much fun. How sweet!

Our last day, it's time to get on the homeward bound bus. After paying our fare we have now a staggering $115 between two of us. Not bad, enough to hold us over for at least the three months at Summer Meadows and maybe all the way to Christmas. Also, I think we can move up to two cokes a day, a just reward for a month in the sun.

THIRD YEAR

September 1958 – September 1959

Chapter 39
Summer Meadows
Grace

Wayside does not provide transportation down state 125 miles away to the State Mental Hospital, Summer Meadows. None of us have our own cars so we have to find at least two people who will take us there! I am going with Amber's father. Eight of us from our class will go with our class and join students from other nursing schools, some even from near-by states. There will be about forty in our group. I am a "C", so I will go with the first group from our class at Wayside.

Excited, I am anxious to get away but wary of what lies ahead. Students who had been there and are now back at Wayside liked the experience, saying, "It is a great change of pace, no "a.m." cares, nor will you be giving out medications or doing treatments. You will just be observing and talking to patients. The classes are interesting, but there are lots of tests." We can never get away from test pressure. It stalks us wherever we go. They told stories about the patients that were interesting and scary. Going into a totally alien world of the mentally ill, I am experiencing some unease for sure.

When we entered the grounds, we were all impressed. Beautiful trees dotted the landscape and large brick buildings were here and there. We followed a map to our residential building. It looked like the other buildings, three floors and a brick step entrance. Students are filing in. Amber and I (we will be roommates) are assigned a room on the top floor. We hurried there and are pleasantly surprised - very spacious with nice furniture and a large closet. The shared bathrooms are down the hall and look very clean and functional. After settling in, we are to report downstairs to the common room. Introductions are done by two staff members and rules are stressed. They are in charge of our safety and gave us pointers about how to protect ourselves on the wards and the grounds. Each of us were given our schedules and our assigned wards for the next morning. Then off to the dining hall we went. The food was plentiful with lots of choices, I stuffed myself. Rumor has it, most students gain 5 to 10 pounds during their stay.

My first assignment is in the men's locked admission ward. All new male patients are channeled through this ward and after a few weeks are sent to either acute or chronic areas. The census at this state hospital is an astonishing 3,502.

Arriving at the assigned building the next morning, four of us were led through one locked ward, then a second locked ward, 1A. We walked down a long hallway with several rooms (like padded cells) on the left with a nurse's office on the right, we entered a large common room that was occupied by about twenty men. Some were sitting at tables, two were lying on the floor, one was pacing up and down the room back and forth, back and forth and some others were standing alone talking to themselves or unseen people, all very strange and alarming. Two men in white suits stood looking over the place, our protectors. Now what? One attendant came over to us and told us to walk around, introduce ourselves to the patients and being careful not to let anyone get behind us. If we wanted we could play card games with those seated around the tables. We were given a set of keys and instructions, "Don't ever leave the ward unlocked, keep the keys with you at all times while on duty. Do not allow the patients access to your keys. They would all like to 'elope' out of here."

During the course of the first morning, I discovered that two patients had been sent by the courts to determine if they are sane and able to stand trial – one accused of murder, the other for repeated assaults on his wife. Nice! There are alcoholics that had been picked up off the streets and others who are suffering from some form of mental illness with potential for violence. I was quite uneasy and reluctant to talk with anyone.

I sat down by a little old man, the only harmless looking one in the room. He was supposed to be coloring, but instead was eating the crayons. After I informed the attendant, the old fellow gave me dirty looks so I moved on to one of the tables and spent the rest of my morning learning to play Black Jack with the alcoholics. They seemed very normal and were very good conversationalists.

When lunch was served the patients were given trays of food with only spoons, (no knives or forks allowed). Some gobbled their food, others ignored the food and one fellow ate all his and started on the unfinished trays of others. He ate so much food that it all came rolling back out all over his shirt and lap. My stomach began churning and I almost joined in. The attendant told me that particular patient does this just to shock the new nurses. He certainly succeeded with me. Maybe "a.m." cares weren't so bad after all. It was a relief to leave for lunch, as if I could eat anything. Following lunch, we went to the resident hall for our first class.

The classes are taught by psychiatrists and other staff. Abnormal Mental Conditions is taught by a youngish man who is a RN. He is the first male nurse I have met. I didn't know men could be nurses. Mr. Davidson, RN, is a very good teacher and his classes are never boring. After two additional classes our first day was over except for homework and studying. Amber and I spent the evening looking over our new Psych books.

So went the days, I was getting use to the wards and there were some sad cases indeed. One young man was very nice looking, clean and friendly and seemed quite normal. Later I found out he was a male prostitute. What? Were there women who visited these men and paid for sex? But no, he was a male prostitute for homosexuals. Who ever heard of such a thing? The world in some places is apparently very weird indeed. I am learning more than I wish to know.

We visited some of the chronic areas. So sad, so many have been there for years and years. They can't go home because there was no longer a home to go to. Some are allowed ground privileges at certain hours. Others never leave the wards. Could anything be more sad?

We assisted with electric shock treatments which are like an electrocution producing seizures. The patients hate them and so do I. The whole thing seems so brutal. However, one man in 1A, who did nothing but lie in a corner for days and days, after receiving several treatments, began to get well. He started to participate and talk with others and amazingly he knew all our names. In a few weeks was well enough to go home. No one seems to know why the treatments work, but they do.

We were told that the effects were discovered quite by accident. A mental patient accidentally endured an electric shock and afterwards showed remarkable improvement. So it was tested and produced amazing results. A rather inhumane way of producing humane results, a reoccurring theme I have discovered exists in many fields of research and medical practice.

The cause of mental illness is a source of great debate. Some believe that the illnesses are caused by a chemical imbalance in the brain or other physical diseases. Others contribute it to trauma and abuse during childhood or other Freudian theories. However, neither theory can be proved scientifically. They lump people according to their symptoms into categories and try to arrive at some consensus or diagnosis and treat accordingly. So much about the human brain is still a mystery. A lot of guessing goes on and none of the doctors seem absolutely sure of anything.

Every illness we studied I thought I might have or be getting after a few weeks in that, forgive the pun, crazy place. I couldn't have been more relieved when the instructor said if one reached the age of nineteen or twenty without symptoms of illness; it was very unlikely to be acquired thereafter. I began to sleep better at night.

So very different from Wayside, I find myself rather liking it and I feel safe because the attendants are at our side immediately if a patient gets out of control and believe me, there were some violent outbursts. On

94

1A, the men often start fights, the attendants are always busy keeping the peace.

One of the attendants told me an amusing story about a psychiatric patient, named Dave, who was standing at the back fence. He was observing a man on the outside changing a flat tire on his car. The man had removed the right rear wheel and removed the lug nuts from the wheel and carefully placed them in the hubcap for safe keeping. The mental patient appeared to make the man nervous and as he was removing the spare tire from the car's trunk, he accidentally knocked the hubcap with the lug nuts into a nearby sewer drain. The man had a puzzled look about him as to how he would go about mounting the spare tire. Dave, noticing the man's predicament offered a suggestion. He said, "Take one lug nut off of each of the three remaining wheels and use them for the missing lug nuts for the spare. Then drive the car slowly to the nearest service station and buy replacements." The man outside the fence was astonished at his suggestion. He said to Dave, "That is a brilliant idea. If you could arrive at that solution, what are you doing in Summer Meadows." Dave replied, "I'm in here because I am crazy, not because I am stupid."

We were given one special assignment, to spend at least eight hours with one patient (at intervals) and record all the conversation and analyze the patient by what we learned regarding his or her diagnosis. By that time I was assigned to a ladies' ward. I picked out a lady who hardly spoke a word. We would sit together in silence, my attempt at conversation ignored. Short case study!

Socially we had some rather good choices. We could ride the bus into a local strip mall and shop or go to the Drive-In Movie Theater with some of the attendants. They liked driving around with the student nurses in their cars. Some girls dated the attendants. We walked into the small town nearby, visited the shops, especially the drug store that had a soda fountain. If we could find a ride we would go home on the weekends, leaving Friday nights and returning Sunday evenings. We had more freedom than at Wayside, no signing in or out and no housemothers. We just needed to be in before the doors were locked for the night.

Seeing and experiencing so much in this odd and bewildering place, I know I'll never forget Summer Meadows. The work was easier but I don't think I will ever want to be a psychiatric nurse, so much bleakness, sadness and so many hopeless cases. I like the brighter side of life. After three months, we headed back to the nurses' home at Wayside. I was ready to return, much wiser and certainly grateful to be re-entering the mostly sane world. Never, ever would I want to be a patient at Summer Meadows, so very different than its name.

Chapter 40
Emergency Nursing
Jo Jo

Finally I'm a senior, there are only eight months left until graduation. The seemingly endless classes are winding down at last. The light is a pinprick at the end of the tunnel. After wading through all the Specialties I have only one left, I can scarcely believe it. Our class in Emergency Nursing is almost over and next Monday three of us will head to the Emergency Room down in the gloomy hospital basement for three weeks.

The head nurse of the ER is Mrs. Rule (a fitting name), a rather slim, trim lady with white hair curling around her head under her cap. She appears to be all business, very professional and for the entire class she taught us she never once cracked a smile (why do head nurses never smile?). She seems to be very serious person. She taught first aid, which included helping the injured and dying, all types of accidents, broken limbs, burns, hemorrhage, etc., etc., both in the ER and out in public places.

Arriving that first Monday morning at 7 a.m., Mrs. Rule was already ruling. She was bossing everyone around and when she saw us her brown eyes seemed to dilate and we braced ourselves to join the other serfs.

One of the graduates, Miss Green, was to take us on tour. In and out of the rooms we went. Surgical rooms, examination rooms, a cast room, waiting room and two patient rooms each occupied by restrained men (alcoholics we were told) one in DTs. He was screaming about bugs crawling around the walls and the other man was loudly snoring, sleeping off one, I suppose. They were apparently too noisy to be up on the other floors. Back down the hall is the morgue with a body covered up waiting for undertakers, Creepy, Creepy. There is also a little room with an autoclave used to sterilize surgical instruments.

Today we are to observe and tomorrow we will be given various assignments. Oh, and yes, since this week we only have one class at 2 p.m., we will be cleaning up all the rooms not in use starting at 12:30 p.m. Do we have the word "maid" tattooed on our foreheads? Wayside couldn't survive without their army of student cleaner uppers.

So we observed and I began some mental note taking. Mrs. Rule it seems, assists the doctors (smiling at them) with minor surgical stuff like cyst removals, suturing up wounds, removal of ingrown toenails, and so on. The other grads place people in rooms, take vital signs, fill out papers, keep check on the waiting room for new walk ins and assist with cast applications. Everyone seems to know what to do. Mrs. Rule runs a tight ship. Two grads will cover the 3-11 shift and low and behold one student nurse will, by herself, cover the night shift. If anyone is carted in or walks in the ER door, we are to phone the night supervisor immediately. Our chores are to busy ourselves cleaning the rooms, autoclaving the instruments, and putting out all necessary supplies for the next day. We are to empty all trash cans and I guess we would be wiping off all the exposed pipes in the hall ceiling if they thought of it. Oh yes, we also are to care for those two alcoholics, giving them their baths before 7 a.m. and all their ordered early "a.m." meds. That one with the DT's, if he is still here, will certainly have a hit and miss bath. Each student will serve one of her three weeks on lovely night duty.

That Thursday, the place was bedlam, several minor surgical procedures were being done and the waiting room full of folks with all kinds of maladies waiting for their turn to be seen. I was in an exam room checking in a bad breather when I heard a lot of running around and shouting. Three ambulances had pulled up and were carting in wounded people. There had been a major auto accident on a highway coming into town. All doctors in the hospital who were able were to report to ER. This was shouted over the hospital's intercom system. I ran out of the room telling the bad breather I would be back. Complete chaos, people were bleeding profusely. One man was lying on a table minus a right foot and Mrs. Rule was applying and releasing a tourniquet around his leg. The doctors flocked in and began assessing and calling out orders. Supervisors showed up, the lab was called and I stood there in awe. They were saving lives right before my eyes and I didn't have a clue about what to do. Two of the injured were soon stabilized and rolled off to surgery, within two hours all were treated and admitted as needed. All eight people survived. These nurses can turn into emergency mode immediately and work together with precision. Their quick action was very impressive.

Would I ever become that efficient? What a challenge! Yes, I liked it in the ER. Never knowing what might happen next but always prepared, always ready, I was intrigued. Maybe this would be my niche.

Eager to learn, I went through the days absorbing everything like a sponge, observing the nurses in different situations. I helped with minor surgeries, application of casts, learned to start IVs and hang blood transfusions. I assessed walk-ins to determine their status, acute patients went before minor things like colds and flu symptoms. Chest pain went straight through. It was all rather fascinating. I didn't even mind the night shift, cleaning and autoclaving. It was all part of getting ready for my future.

Big dreams might be realized if I stay the course. Two and one half years I have been ordered around and been on the cleanup crew. With more time behind than before, all the mundane tasks are easier to put up with. I am proceeding carefully learning everything I can and someday, maybe, just maybe, I might have a job like Mrs. Rule, head nurse in an Emergency Department somewhere. That would be so cool; walking around in my uniform, ready for any emergency, barking out commands, assisting the doctors and impressing everyone with my expertise and efficiency. Unlike Mrs. Rule, I would be smiling at everyone.

Chapter 41
Christmas Tree, Oh Christmas Tree
Reva

It's Christmas time and our last one at Wayside Nursing School. Reva and I have out schedules and we both work Christmas Eve and Christmas Night – last shift. "So I'll be Home for Christmas", will be only in our dreams. How will we endure being here on that very family holiday?

We decided, we will just have to celebrate our own way, so we will put up a Christmas tree in our room. Reva's home is close to the woods, so her two days off this week she will have her Daddy cut a very small tree to bring back and I will bring some ornaments from Grandma's.

Arriving at the nurses' home a few days before Christmas, I watched Reva come up the front walk with her tree. I met her at the front lobby door and back we went to our room. The decorations that I brought included some cut-out snow flakes for the window, tree ornaments, and some garlands. We added some string popcorn (no lights allowed) for a nice finishing touch. The tree was lovely, our room looked so festive.

All during the day, girls stopped by and raved about our tree and accompanying decorations. We shared some cookies that Reva's mother had sent.

That night, reluctantly we left our dear tree and went off to work at the hospital. On the way out the downstairs side door, I paused to check the notices on the bulletin board. I read, "No live Christmas trees allowed this year. Ordered by the Fire Safety Commissioner." Reva and I looked at each other. Well there goes our tree. We will take it down tomorrow after we wake up.

That morning I almost fell into bed, eight hours on 2 South was a killer, and Reva followed me. She worked 2 North and never even got to the cafeteria for a late supper break. We were dead to the world in minutes.

About four hours later, I was awakened by someone pounding on our door, I rolled out of bed. It was Mrs. Woods, one of the assistant house mothers. She said, "You both are to report to Mrs. River's office." "What for?" I questioned. "I don't know, but you two need to get over there immediately," she replied.

Had we done something terrible at work? No, really, all had gone well. Had something happened with our families? That wasn't likely if we both are called over. Dazed with sleep, we hurried to get dressed, brushed our teeth and combed our hair as quickly as possible. We know better than to appear at Mrs. River's office in a shabby state.

I have never seen a person so angry. She was on her feet as we walked in the doorway. "This is deliberate mutiny", she yelled. "It has been reported to me that you have a live Christmas tree in your room. Which of you brought that tree into the nurses' home?" Reva spoke in a very quiet voice, "I did Mrs. Rivers", and she tried to explain about the notice that we didn't see. Mrs. Rivers refused to listen. She shrieked and raved at us, shouted about fire safety and again – "deliberate mutiny." I thought she was about to pop her cork, so to speak. You would think that the nurses' home was nothing but a heap of smoldering ashes. After about ten minutes of verbal abuse (it seemed like an eternity), she sent us from the room promising that the student council would meet to determine our punishment and shouted, "Get that tree down immediately." What a Scrooge!

A grim Christmas this would be indeed. Reva and I worked two more nights before the blow fell. I would be "campused" for six weeks and if no more infractions, restrictions would be lifted. Reva, however would be suspended for six weeks to begin immediately because she brought in the offending tree. She would be required to return for classes and make up the six weeks duty work after graduation. No credit hours for classes attended. She would be allowed to attend graduation but would not be finished making up the six weeks in time to take state boards with the remainder of the class in October. The next testing session would be in January.

Reva was angry and crushed. This was terribly unfair. Who reported us? No one had been in our room but our fellow students and friends. Also wasn't the punishment unusually severe for Reva? No appeal to Mrs. Rivers helped. Reva went home.

I couldn't understand it. Some students had made medicine mistakes and other worse things. Why was Reva treated so harshly? It seems that our superiors were always out to get her. I never hated this place more than I did that day. Alone in our room my heart broke for Reva. Never, ever did I have a better friend. She had lifted my spirits so many times with her humor and encouragement. One could always trust her, she would never betray a friend and she doesn't have a vindictive bone in her body, pretty, witty, and high spirited. Who did this and why?

We stayed in touch over the days ahead and I kept my ears open. A regular Miss Marple, I asked questions here and there. Finally it came out, a member of the council, one of our closest friends (we thought) reported her because after all, a rule was broken, one that could have dire consequences if there were a fire.

How could I tell Reva? Betrayed by her friend. We were seniors. When did we become so concerned with the breaking of crazy, ridiculous rules? What has happened? The one for all, all for one glue had dissolved. Somehow, someone was very impressed with their own importance. I guess if you are voted in to serve on student council you must swing your weight around and agree with such a stern reprimand. How hurt Reva would be. The whole incident reminds me of a verse I read in the Bible the other day.

Psalm 55:12-14
For it is not my enemy who reproaches
me. Then I could bear it.
Nor is it one who hates me who has exalted himself against
me. Then I could hide myself from him.
But it is you my equal
My companion and familiar friend
We who had sweet fellowship together
Walked in the house of God in the throng.

I am not like Reva, vindictive I am. I met up with Karen (our supposed friend) and told her in no certain terms what I thought of her betrayal. She answered me "Incidents like that need to be reported and I never dreamed the council and administration would come down so hard on Reva. For that I am very sorry. The council and grads agreed, Reva must be made an example to deter other outrageous behavior and complete disrespect for authority." I felt like throwing up.

Some days later, after much stewing in my mind, I talked to Reva and told her the awful truth. She was shocked but took the news in stride. After all this she was more determined than ever to graduate.
"Someday, when this is all behind us, the whole event will be just a little bump in life's rocky road," she said.

Two weeks later, while on suspension, Reva met and fell madly in love with a great guy who lived not far from her little hometown. A spring wedding is being planned; she is in a blissful bubble. That was just like Reva, never giving in and never giving up. A modern day Scarlet O'Hara, she shared Scarlet's philosophy, "After all, tomorrow is another day."

Chapter 42
Here, There and Everywhere
Feona

Our last year! We have finished most of our classes and all the specialties. Now we are being scheduled all over Wayside, filling in where staff is low, mostly for a two week period of time. Somehow, I have been teamed with Jill and we are going from one Med-Surg floor to another. I have been counting off the months; October, November, December, and so forth. Now it is the first day of April and we are beginning our second week on 2 North. We need our skates. The assignments are written for Superwoman.

First item on duty is to write down our assignment. So Jill and I are copying down ours. Well, this is even worse than anything from last week. Jill whispered, "Feona, look at this. We have the temps for the whole hall and eight patients instead of six. I have a four patient ward and two semi- privates. Can you believe this? I am to get Mrs. Nichols up in a wheelchair and she is in a hip-spika cast." This cast was applied for a fractured hip and covers the body from the upper chest, all the way down the affected hip and leg, just below the knee on the other leg with a bar between the knees to hold the hip in place. There is an opening at the buttocks and between the legs so the patient can use the bedpan. There is no bending of the body, the patient lies flat for usually six weeks. This is indeed a challenge and Jill looks frantic. I assured her, "Don't worry, we will work together and somehow figure it out. If they said get Mrs. Nichols up we will do it or die."

I noticed the clinical instructors were looking at us rather strangely. Walking over to us one said, "Why aren't you two saying anything about your assignment?" Looking at her, I said, "Why? Should we say something? Did you all forget to add something?" They both looked disgusted. Mrs. Sanders said, "Don't you girls recognize an April Fool's joke when you see one? The duties we wrote for you are impossible to complete." Surprised, Jill said, "You mean I don't have to get Mrs. Nichols up in a wheelchair?" They looked at us like we were idiots. Didn't they understand? Our assignments are always horrendous on this floor. There was little difference between this day and any other. Who are the April Fools here?

On to 4 North, seniors we are and we have become very efficient at getting our "a.m." cares done on time. So we decided to be nice. We would help out those poor first year students who were having such a struggle. Off we go, finishing up our six patients a piece, we helped make beds, clean bedside stands, fill water pitchers and numerous other tasks for the "Probies" for two whole weeks. Next week we would go to "Peds."

The clinical instructors set us down that last day to read our evaluations and Jill and I knew it would be one of our best. We were taken aback to read such things as, "works poorly with others, doesn't follow instructions, doesn't take charge when necessity arises," and for me "often breaks out in boisterous, annoying laughter, very unbecoming for an inspiring professional nurse." This was truly shocking.

Jill looked at me in astonishment and said, "I simply must refuse to sign this. It's so untrue. Were they even observing us?"

Refusing to sign means big trouble. Number one, we are questioning the opinion of our superiors; and number two, it will mean a session with Mrs. Rivers, who isn't about to take our part.

"Jill," I said, "You are right, it is a lie to even agree with them. However, we need to think this through. We are seniors with only a few months left. Do we really want to stir up the pot? Let's not allow those CI's to put us in jeopardy. Next week we will be somewhere else and maybe, just maybe, we can balance this out with a good report."

Jill reluctantly agreed. "It's actually supporting an outright lie, but you are right. We must for once think about what is best for us. If we have learned anything, it's keep a low profile and don't upset the higher ups."

So sign it we did. When the CI's came to collect them, they added a few nasty verbal remarks. We sat there like little obedient slaves, taking the lashes without complaint. They looked so self-righteous. Had they ever been students?

Here, there and everywhere we go, plowing through for those last months. We can and will endure most everything now, just pile it on. The finish line gets closer each day and now it is within sight.

Chapter 43
A Country Wedding
Reva

Getting married! Six months ago that was the last thing on my mind. I didn't even have a boyfriend instead I thought I was fated to be the "other woman", for Pete's sake!

After that terrible Christmas Tree incident, I found myself sitting at home. Mother and Daddy both thought the whole thing absurd and ridiculous, but we could do nothing but ride it out. However, God works in mysterious ways because I met David and everything changed. After dating for about two months he proposed and being head over heels, I accepted and we began to make plans!

The wedding will be in April. My suspension will be over and I will have less than six months to go so the marriage ban will be lifted. Not only that, I won't have to stay at the Nurses' Home another day but will be able to drive into Wayside for any remaining classes and hospital duty in David's car!

Mother is all aflutter and busy with satin and lace sewing my wedding gown. David asked Daddy for my hand in marriage (believe me, he is getting more than my hand). Daddy said "yes" but I must promise to finish my training and graduate. So promised.

We are planning a very simple country wedding with a reception in the church basement, punch, mints, nuts and wedding cake will be served. My sister will be my matron-of-honor. Jill, Feona, and Susie will be my bridesmaids, dressed in lacy spring colored dresses, pink, blue and light green. Rachel's Aunt Mae (who is a seamstress), has agreed to make the dresses. It is all so terribly exciting.

David is wonderful, so tall and handsome. From what I hear, girls have been after him for years, but he was never serious about any. I don't understand it at all, we just clicked. I met him at a high school basketball game that I went to with my brother one evening. I was so bored being at home and I missed the girls at Wayside and a few were going to be at the game. David and I met there, were introduced and it all began. We just had to see each other almost everyday after that, could anything be crazier?

We found this darling apartment in David's hometown and I am dreaming of how I will dress it up to make it ours; lots of soft throw pillows, colorful rugs and indoor plants. Wayside is <u>far</u> in the back of my mind. I just want to keep my promise to Daddy. Old Mrs. Rivers and all those other staff nurses who have been so mean can go fly kites.

When I told Jill, Feona and Susie I wanted them for bridesmaids, they danced around the room. We are all wedding mad (is that a real condition?). There are five other girls in our class who are planning to marry soon. One was already hitched last October, eloped! Now she thinks she must have a proxy wedding so she won't get a bad reference from Wayside for lying and cheating. Not only that, she is three months along (pregnant). How will she explain the dates to her child when he or she is a teenager?

I walked down the aisle that Friday evening at 7 p.m. The organ was playing and flickering candles made the church look solemn and lovely. Due to the candlelight, one couldn't see the old faded pew coverings and the cracks on some of the walls. Some major overhauling is long overdue. So what, my eyes were on David standing down there looking like a movie star. I'm not sure I know how to be a wife, but I intend to give it my best shot. It shouldn't be too difficult; females have been doing it for centuries.

After the ceremony, greeting all the guests at the door, putting in an appearance at the reception, cutting the cake and we were waving goodbye. I hope my sister and mother will take it upon themselves to serve the wedding cake. David and I, now husband and wife (that sounds strange), have to get out of here. We only have a week and David is back to work and it is a return to Wayside for me. My once dreaded, but surprisingly, wonderful suspension will be over.

Chapter 44
Public Health and All that Jazz
Pauline

Boring! Boring! Miss Walls has scheduled folks from the County Public Health Department to come here and teach us about all the clinics that they have to serve the public. Two weeks have passed so far in the class (30 hours) and six different Public Health workers have stood before us and spouted off. Who cares if they clean teeth, go to school to give vaccinations and search for head lice. They investigate any report of infectious diseases, even quarantine houses if someone within has scarlet fever or some other serious infectious disease. Apparently they go around snooping and making a nuisance of themselves.

The silliest one of all was the man who gave us a lecture on pasteurized milk; a little gray haired man in a very untidy, dirty looking gray suit, in need of a shave, shoes badly soiled and he would spit when he talked. He spoke in a low monotone which caused a collective yawn. None of our instructors happened to be in the room so things got quickly out of hand. No attention was paid to him as we talked and giggled. Reva (now married) was sitting up very straight, not participating in the riotous behavior, but reading a novel, looking up often with an interested look on her face. He babbled along about boiling milk to a certain necessary temperature, more or less talking to himself. Then appearing very annoyed, he stopped and said loudly, "If the rest of you young ladies would show some manners and pay attention like your clinical instructor is doing over there, you might learn important things about milk", looking right at Reva. Well, that did it. Hysterical uproarious laughter filled the room. Reva stood up and said, "Alright girls, your behavior is appalling. Stop at once or you will be marched over to Mrs. River's office. Now, Mr. Wright I suppose we should call it a day with this lecture. None of the students boil milk but we are totally in agreement with the pasteurization process." He picked up his notes and marched out of the room and we all gathered around Reva, still laughing, thanking her for quick thinking and boredom relief. We were all praying that he went straight out of the building, not stopping to talk with anyone. Thankfully we never heard anything about that class from the higher ups.

We also were assigned to attend certain clinics for the very poor, held at the Health Department. I was to go to a prenatal one and assist the doctor in his physical examinations. Dr. Detrick was attending these ladies. Vital signs, weight, fetal heart tones were assessed, also a general physical and pelvic exam. One girl, who looked no more than sixteen, was up on the table. He told her to open her mouth. "Now Miss Macey, do you see this young ladies' teeth? You can almost always determine if a patient is on welfare due to the complete disregard they have for their dental health." I couldn't believe it. Did he think she was deaf? How could he be so thoughtless? The poor thing had tears in her eyes and if I had enough nerve, I would have given him a swift kick. I'm glad he was looking in her mouth and not mine. I have a cavity beginning in one of my molars and I am in hopes that it doesn't get larger so I can get it fixed as soon as I finish and start to work. I suppose he was never poor or if he once was he has forgotten.

When I reached eighteen, Mom no longer received Social Security benefits for me, just a small widow's pension. She explained to me, "I have tried everything but I cannot come up with $65 for your second year tuition. You will have to drop out of training. I am so sorry." Oh no, not after enduring that entire first year. I was devastated. Somehow one of the charitable clubs in town got wind of my plight and they paid the bill for me or I wouldn't be standing by Dr. Detrick today. Even if someday I am flushed with money. I pray I'll never forget that poor pregnant girl as she lay there absorbing such verbal insensitivity.

Many of the lessons learned at nursing school do not come from textbooks. Maybe I should have been more sensitive to the feelings of that "Public Health Pasteurized Milk" person too.

Chapter 45
Achieving the Achievement Tests
Katie

Miss Walls is all in a stir. We have been given Achievement Tests that are the exact format of the state boards, the tests we must pass in order to become Registered Nurses. The majority have done poorly. The grades we made were sent home along with the grades from our regular classes. There was a comment added, asking our parents or guardians to encourage us to study more so when the Achievement Tests are repeated, we could at least pass.

Miss Walls stomped around the classroom, waving papers and shouting, "I just don't understand, we have been teaching you girls for almost three years. Are you all unteachable or just lazy? We have tried our best to make nurses of you. Even your duty evaluations have not been what we have hoped. For the next month you will be required to attend review classes then we will repeat the tests. Get those books out and get to work. Your class will be the worst ever at State Boards."

Oh, great! Now we will be going to classes about classes and taking those tests again will be a real pain. They are always on our case.

Dad was upset with me too when he received that letter in the mail. He never calls long distance unless there is a dire emergency and the phone rang for me that evening. "What happened?" he shouted in the phone. "How could you have only made a six when there were fifty questions? Did we spend all that money for nothing?"

What explanation could I give? We never had a test in that format before and I made a mess of it. There was no way to appease my Dad and he wouldn't listen to my lame excuses. I tried, "Everyone did poorly, we were taken by surprise. I am terrible at taking timed tests." All of this said, he continued to go on about how disappointed he was. My stepmother got on the phone and she said, "Now Katie, you know your dad, he will calm down. Don't worry, just keep studying. I have faith in your abilities and I know next time we will get a better report." Helen always is so supportive and I am determined to improve. Those boards are coming up in the fall and I must be ready.

We all dug out our books and old tests and crammed like crazy for four days. When I get out of here I swear, I'm not going to open another medical book for years. Bring on the novels.

The classes were intense. Mrs. Caskey even had some of the doctors over for review. It seems Wayside will fold if we fail State Boards. Something about a reflection on the whole place.

The second round went much better, but not up to expectations, so we had to endure two more weeks with Mrs. Caskey snapping and blinking her little beady eyes at us. All this carrying on almost made me want to fail just to irritate all the agitated teaching staff, including Mrs. Rivers, who made a visit to just to voice her disgust for our poor showing.

Now it is all up to us. No more review of the reviews. They have more or less washed their hands of us. Our last classes are over and summer duty starts next week. I have June off and I can't wait to get away. I'll pack up all the books and open some every day, Dad will be looking. My prayer is "O Lord, let me pass state boards. I don't want to disappoint my whole family and break my dad's heart."

WAYSIDE HOSPITAL SCHOOL OF NURSING
Date   June 1, 1958

FINAL GRADES FOR SCHOOL TERM ENDING   _JUN_1, 1958
KATIE_HATTER

Subject	Grade	Subject	Grade
Anatomy	B	Medical Nursing I, II	85,85
Microbiology	C	Communicable Disease Nursing	75
Chemistry	B	Tuberculosis Nursing	79
Psychology	85	Dermatology	
Sociology	75	Surgical Nursing I, II	80,81
History of Nursing	82	Emergency Nursing	
Professional Adjustments I	C+	Orthopedics	78
Professional Adjustments II		Eye, Ear, Nose and Throat	88
Nursing – Elementary	81	Urology	78
Drugs and Solutions	86	Obstetric	85
Pharmacology	84	Pediatrics	78
Nutrition, Foods	80	Psychiatry	90
Diet Therapy	87	Public Health Nursing	
		Endocrine	
Nursing Arts Advanced	86	English 405	B
Case Study Method	75	Clinical Instruction – O.R. Dept	
Introduction to Med Sciences	75	Nursing of Newborn	78
Physiology	C	Gynecological Nursing	85
Neurological Nursing	88		

ACHIEVMENT TEST RESULTS FOR FOLLOWING SUBJECTS: Anatomy & Physiology **17**; Pharmacology **06**;   Nursing of Children **24**;   Obstetrics Nursing **38**

   REMARKS: Students not averaging a 50 percentile in each of the Achievement tests taken, will be required to take the test over again, therefore your daugh
   ter will have to take Anatomy and Physiology, Pharmacology, Nursing of Children and Obstetrics Nursing. Would suggest that you encourage your daughter to study these subjects so she will be able to pass these tests.
Final grade report

   Mrs. Charlotte W. Rivers R.N
Director of Nurses

Chapter 46
Our Last Summer Here
Rachel

Forty hours a week for eight more weeks plus one month off and graduation will be here. Some of the girls have already moved out and have transportation so they can travel in for their shift from their homes. Six are now married. I have no other transportation except walking and my home is two miles away so I will be at the Nurses' Home until the end. I sometimes walk home if I'm on day duty just to visit my mother. This place has become rather empty and lonely. Not like before with everyone running in and out and so much going on.

This evening I'm taking Katie and Jill home with me for dinner. Jill misses Reva a lot. She married in April. We all went to her little country church to see the wedding. It's so nice to see Reva happy. She was treated so badly. We are all facing lots of changes and not any too soon for sure. I'm more than ready to quit this place.

Katie is now finishing up three weeks in newborn nursery so the staff nurses can have vacation. Jill is over at "cysto" (where kidney and bladder tests are done) for this week and I am trotting up and down 2 South doing those endless "a.m." cares. We can work extra hours (relief) for 75 cents an hour. I have done some of this, but I'm so tried and it is all so monotonous. I'm a clock watcher, most happy to get off duty and not eager to add to those grueling forty hours. Mother tells me that I should take my time off for rest and renewal. I can earn money when I have an actual nursing job. Glad to agree, I run home as much as possible.

Last week I was working the 3 to 11 shift. We had a loud, crazy patient and he was placed in a private room down the hall. Amazingly, he pried the window open and escaped, dropping down ten feet to the ground. We don't know how long he was gone before the medicine girl went in his room. She discovered him missing and sounded the alarm. Such a fuss you never did see, security, the hospital administrator, Mrs. Rivers, and the city police were notified. Somewhere a man, gone mad, in just a hospital gown was loose in the city. His family was notified and they were causing a great stir (no wonder). Difficult it was to keep my mind on the tasks at hand, two enemas and four wound changes. Finally, before eleven o'clock came, they found him at the local high school at their empty football field, sitting on the bleachers calmly smoking a cigarette. Thankfully it was a warm night. I supposed he just wanted to have a smoke. What a relief! The hospital's administration was in a tangle – law suit, law suit, must be churning around in their heads.

Needless to say, there will be some serious debates coming up. I am glad that I wasn't the charge nurse that night, an incident report concerning losing a patient. I wouldn't want to write that up and have to sign my name to such an alarming incident.

Mother welcomed us with a smile and a table full of food, ham and green beans with fresh sliced tomatoes. The strawberries were in, so she made strawberry shortcake with mounds of whipped cream accompanied by a wonderful cup of tea. A lovely time was had by all, never did a girl have a kinder, more thoughtful mother.

Later that evening we walked back to the nurses' home. Even now, if we live there, we have to sign in before curfew. We are now twenty one years old! None of us will miss the constant supervision. Some of us are already assuming graduate nurse duties. How silly it is to still be treated like first year students.

Jill, Katie and I had already signed on for jobs at Wayside. Jill to Pediatrics, Katie to Delivery Room and I am going to work on 4 North, my very favorite, Med-Surg floor. The floor is at least fifty feet from the ground. Hopefully I will be unlikely to lose a patient out the window.

We all are crossing off the days. At last, at last, baring some major disaster, I believe we three are going to make it.

It's the summer of our Senior Year, almost finished! No one can possibly be happier than I! The name "student nurse" is getting very old. For so long the journey has seemed endless, but now the end is in sight.

However, we are now all in crisis mode. An outbreak of polio has hit our area and victims are coming in. They enter the "ER" with elevated temp, fatigue, nausea and vomiting and some with worse symptoms; stiff neck, headache and muscle weakness. They are then moved to the isolation wing and some of us are being called over for duty.

Dr. Hemmingway has had special training in treating infected patients and other physicians are calling on him to diagnosis their patients and aid in preparing private duty, graduate and nursing students to care for this onslaught.

For many years this disease has been greatly feared because it mostly effects children and can cause death and if not death, mild to severe paralysis of various muscle groups. It used to be called Infantile Paralysis. Since then the virus has been isolated and a vaccine has been developed but many still have not received the vaccine. A nationwide campaign called "the March of Dimes" is held every year so funds can be available for research and treatment. We students have all been immunized. So far, Grace, Pauline, Feona and I have been sent to the isolation unit.

We have six patients with the diagnosis and we are watching them very carefully for any symptoms that especially affect the breathing. We have them several days in isolation until the acute phase is over. This is mostly a one-on-one vigil and I am watching over Charlie.

Charlie has come in from one of the rural areas, a small town called Kolesville. It seems the breakouts all occur in hot weather and some think the virus is picked up in swimming pools. I don't think Kolesville has a swimming pool. Charlie is eight years old and such a sweet, scared little fellow. After a few hours I began to notice some changes. His temperature was spiking and he was having trouble swallowing liquids and then he began having some trouble breathing. I put the call light on and a graduate nurse came in, looked at Charlie, went out and called for Dr. Hemmingway. He came in the room, read my notes and examined the little patient. The next thing I knew some orderlies were moving things around in the room and then in came the iron lung, a long round tube-like structure with doors and gauges on it and a hole at the front. In went Charlie with just his head sticking out of the front opening on a little shelf with a pillow. They plugged it in and set the gauges and it began with its positive and negative pressure causing Charlie to breathe. So scary, I believe if anyone looked at me they would see me shaking, but all eyes were on Charlie. Dr. Hemmingway looked around at us and began to teach us how to operate the darn thing. The small doors must be opened quickly and carefully to tend to this little body. You also must open and slam one of the doors every half hour to cause Charlie to sigh or cough to prevent pneumonia and the doctor gave a lot of other instructions that had my head spinning. Charlie was listening too, wide eyed with tears rolling down his little cheeks that he couldn't even wipe away. The parents were weeping in the hallway. It was a scene I will never forget. One of the private duty nurses was pulled over from another patient and took over the nursing duties. I was to stay in the room however, to learn from her and assist. There were no atheists about. Everyone was praying for that dear little boy. If only the vaccine had reached his small town.

After the news about the outbreak hit the air waves and newspapers, an outright panic occurred. People were lining up everywhere getting the vaccine. It was rushed into every small town, rural areas, schools, fire stations, and post offices. It was too late for the fifteen that came to Wayside. When the isolation ward was full other patients were transferred in ambulances to other hospitals and one even in an iron lung was taken away in a big truck to a nearby city. There were two deaths and some had paralysis of mostly their legs. One young girl eighteen years old would need assistance with breathing the rest of her life. Some patients faired much better and had no apparent lasting side effects.

But what about Charlie? We watched over him for four seemingly endless days and then I began to notice a change. The iron lung's gauge began jumping around and acting strangely. Full of panic, I looked at Mrs. Brown (the private duty nurse on my shift) and she immediately began adjusting the machine and said "Well, how about that! Charlie is fighting the iron lung with his own breathing." The doctor was notified and after coming in and observing Charlie, he said, "Let's begin to wean him off, every thirty minutes turn the machine off for five minutes and if all goes well we will continue to increase the off time."

Little by little we increased the off time and in twenty four hours Charlie was breathing on his own. We were able to take him out of the iron lung and the little guy was so happy. Not only that he could move everything and seemed to have no paralysis, only some muscle weakness in the left leg. Dr. Hemmingway said Charlie should make a complete recovery. Well, you would think the circus had come to town. His family was elated. They brought in balloons and his very favorite toys. The nurses called the cafeteria and we all had a cake and ice cream celebration. No words are known that could express everyone's relief. Charlie's father, right there in the room, thanked us all with tears on his cheeks and believe it or not, he offered up a grateful thanks to God right there for answering all our prayers.

After all that, Charlie held on to his Captain Ranger toy with one hand and dove into his ice cream with the other and seemed to wonder what was going on. He then said, "Mom, I am really glad to be out of that crazy place. I never again want anyone else to wipe my nose or brush my teeth. Tell me why was everyone in the room all covered up? I could only see their eyes. With all that slamming and noise from that crazy thing I could hardly sleep. It this what you meant a few weeks ago when I heard you whisper to Dad that Aunt Louise had to be taken to the crazy house? I bet she didn't like it either."

What a happy day! Somehow it helps make up for so many other times when there are no happy endings.

An exhausting and difficult time those few weeks were that summer. Finally the outbreak ended. We had no more polio admissions and everyone, I'm sure, was much relieved. Dr. Hemmingway was tireless, sometimes at the hospital all night, and the nurses, how they kept vigil, endless hours on their feet. But most of all, I remember Charlie, the little boy in the iron lung who lived through one of the most alarming diseases that attacks little ones. He never would have made it without the doctors and nurses of Wayside. I'm grateful that I was there helping some and was included in Charlie's happy recovery celebration.

Chapter 48
Gathering the Proof
Katie

For almost three years now I have been collecting souvenirs from everywhere to help me remember nursing school. Just last week, I was sent back to surgery for two weeks. Going there was not what I wanted, but who cares what I want? Surprisingly it was much easier the second time, going in with previous knowledge, I was all prepared, if I could just get lucky and not have to scrub for "Old Red Hood." I did get to scrub for my favorite doctor and I carefully watched when he removed his sterile gloves and put them in the carryout trash container. I was able to snatch one out and add it to my stash.

I have time schedules, notices of rule changes, a program from our capping ceremony, newspaper articles about Wayside, a student nurse's admission handbook, a printout of my grades (not very good). I have gathered items from all of the specialties, a new born bracelet (made by me) from beads in the delivery room, and a card with the number of deliveries that I scrubbed for there. From "Peds" I have my first work assignment sheet, a little knitted booty and a tiny spoon. From Summer Meadows I have a dried leaf from one of the beautiful old oak trees, a wax imprint of one of the keys to C2 – a ward I was assigned to and also my first test score. I made a grade of ninety percent (my one and only in almost three years).

Anyhow I have a whole pile of stuff and I intended to buy some scrapbooks with my first paycheck and preserve all the memories to remind me of my time in prison.

The girls think I'm crazy. They say things like, "Who would want to remember this place? We don't want any reminders. We just want to forget the whole miserable time."

However, I know how it is with memories. Someday they will come to me with a request to see my scrapbooks. This experience has been very rough at times but we have had good times too. The laughter - we will remember for sure and we can now laugh at ourselves. Also our time together was unique and not shared by many girls our age.

I saved a few things from our parties and even though only a few of us have cameras, I was able to borrow Dad's and I have some nice shots from our St. Patrick's Day celebration eating green spaghetti. I also have a photo of the nurse's home before the new wing was added. Dad told me he would get lots of film for graduation so I will have more photos to add.

After my last day as a student I plan to pick out a student uniform that has survived, the one most intact and keep it. Jo Jo told me she was pitching hers out, she is only interested in the all white ones. I'm keeping one, if for no other reason I will be able to prove when the middle age spread arrives that I had a twenty inch waistline.

I have a letter I'm keeping from one of the girls who left during our second year. It reads as follows;

Dear Katie:

I am sorry that I left without explaining to you the reason for my departure, Mom picked me up and I had to leave quickly. She had to have the car back home in time for Dad to leave for work.

I just couldn't take it anymore. Once I got to surgery, everything seemed to go wrong. After a terrible morning scrubbing in surgery for "Red Hood" (who called me stupid, dumb and other mean things), Pauline and I did surgical preps all evening. The list was long and it took us three hours to finish. The next morning, Pauline and I were called into one of the operating rooms where one of our "preps" was draped for surgery. The bright overhead light was on and a few missed hairs were shockingly visible plus we forgot to clean out the patient's belly button (navel is the correct word). The staff was having a fit and one grad demonstrated her displeasure when several dried chunks were extracted from said belly button.

Later that day the clinical instructor called us into a corner for a conference. Our punishment was "preps" every night for one whole week and two weeks "campused"!

I phoned Mom crying and begging her to let me leave. She said, "Those people there are crazy. Pack up your things, I will be there in an hour."

I am so glad to be home. I hated, being there, I really did. I hope to see you again sometime. You were a good friend.

Love,
Tammy

I can understand perfectly why she gave up. The punishment far out weighed the crime. Pauline hung in there, however and took it like a trooper. I am glad they didn't force her out too. She was even laughing about the whole dumb incident the other day.

One thing important about my collecting, I will have proof of what really happened. If anyone should say in the future, "Oh, all that can't be true, you girls are exaggerating. No one would tolerate such treatment." I will be there with my scrapbooks with the truth spilling off the pages.

Let's see, I need to get this stuff in some sort of order, categorized by time and date will be the best plan.

Chapter 49
What We Now Know
Grace

Summer 1959, I feel like a top that was wound up very tight and let go. I have been spinning for three years and now I'm beginning to come to a stop. Two weeks of hospital duty left then graduation! Amazing it is when I consider how little I knew when I arrived here. Few were any previous hospital visits at Wayside. My family is so far very healthy. That distinctive hospital smell doesn't bother me anymore and "a.m." cares seem easy compared to the difficult time I had in the beginning.

Now I know about Surgery, Obstetrics, Pediatrics, Diet Kitchen, Psychiatric Nursing, Newborns, Emergency Nursing, "Cysto" and more. I can give out meds, start IVs, give blood transfusions, insert nasal gastric tubes, assist with spinal taps and the placement of chest tubes. I can also tube feed adults and newborns. I have learned about hundreds of medications, dosage and side effects, lab tests and how to interpret lab results, how to deal with doctors (some of the time), how to plan work more efficiently, how to anticipate needs and when to notify doctors, how to interpret vital signs, take care of patients in isolation and iron lungs and how to be a charge nurse. I have done hundreds of treatments such as enemas, catherizations, wound dressings, including care of burns. One of the OB doctors actually allowed me to deliver a baby. I could go on and on and yet I also know I have only scratched the surface when it comes to all there is to know about the world of medicine.

All of us have grown up and at lighting speed. No time for much reflection, we moved forward in survival mode and changed from wide-eyed innocents to young career nurses. A transformation I wouldn't have believed possible but it happened to all who held on for dear life through all those twists and turns. We will soon be professionals and will leave our silliness at the hospital door and at last be adults.

Last evening some of us gathered together in Jo Jo's room and talked about what is ahead. We will actually become wage earners and lots of plans were voiced as to what we will do when we have our own money. Most everyone wants a car. Me, I can walk to my job at Wayside so I am heading for the shops with the first pay and reward myself with some new clothes. Also, a trip to the beauty shop will be nice. Someone else can do my hair and nails for a change. It's all so exciting; graduation, state boards, and freedom, sweet, sweet freedom! No moral police watching our every move.A celebration was in order so we decided to go down to the Rec Room for one last party. Making toasts with cokes; we ate candy bars and

119

chips. We danced to the worn out records and sang and laughed a lot. Of course there will be challenges ahead, but the important thing we learned is that we are survivors. I wish everyone who started out could be here all together for one last time. Memories flooded my mind about those early days. We were just kids trying to find our way. Anyone who spends three years here and comes out alive is better prepared for the unknown future than most twenty- one year olds.

I'm glad I came here but most of all, I'm glad it's nearly over. "We have finished the course, we have kept the faith."

<u>Wayside School of Nursing</u>

Commencement Exercises

Friday evening, September the fourth

Nineteen hundred and fifty nine

At eight o'clock p.m.

West End High School Auditorium

Chapter 50
Congratulations - Graduate
Lindsay

All morning I have been packing my bags not worrying about what to pack because this one last time everything goes. My last few hours here at the Nurses' Home and I'm out of this place at last. Never did I think this day would come. What a blessed relief! Finished! Finished! My final day working as a student was two days ago. Yesterday we were off duty to rehearse for our graduation ceremony.

Graduation was held over at the local high school at eight p.m. That very day we were given three all white uniforms and we would wear one to the ceremony. They presented us also with a lovely Wayside Hospital Nursing School pin, shaped like a cross with the hospital logo on it, our initials and year of graduation was etched on the back.

The auditorium was filled with parents, siblings, relatives, friends, nursing students, graduate nurses, our teachers and administrative staff. Some of the doctors were even there. We walked in single file to "Pomp and Circumstance" in our white uniforms, our caps on our heads with a single black band attached, a very special moment. We took our seats on the stage and the ceremony began. Prayers and speakers, Mrs. Rivers gave a little talk. She looked very relieved, another class out the door, so to speak. Especially our class, the teachers and staff often reminded us about how troublesome we were, the worst class in recent memory. We all rattled that Nightingale Pledge again, not much better than at the capping ceremony, Mrs. Rivers frowned. Mr. Morehouse, the hospital administrator stood and began handing out the diplomas as Miss Walls called out each name. When my name was called I walked over and received my diploma and it read, "Lindsay Hinkle (HAS COMPLETED THE NURSING SCHOOL PROGRAM)." It was signed by some important people. Holding the end of three years of difficult, anxiety filled days in my hands, I just couldn't help it, the tears came. I felt almost numb with joy. After all these precious documents were handed out the audience clapped and cheered. Some special awards were presented (I didn't get one) but that didn't matter one bit, then we were all presented with a beautiful red rose and we marched out, diplomas and rose in hand. Happy, happy time!

After graduation we took lots of pictures and then went on to a reception in our honor, yes, in our honor at the nurses' home. Soft drinks, tea, cookies and punch were served and we walked around shaking hands and smiling at our former adversaries and tormentors. You could tell they really were happy for us and I suppose proud of themselves for whipping us into some kind of nurse-like shape. My mother glowed and my dad looked like he might pop his buttons. A good time was had by all.

Now I am outside with my bags and my parents are helping me pack up their car. Some of the other girls are hurrying out and soon the class of 1959 will be on to another phase in our lives. The staff of Wayside offered everyone jobs, but only about fourteen of us are staying. Others are spreading out in all directions. One girl is going to college to get her nursing degree. Feona and Suzy are heading off to California to find jobs there.

Pausing for a few minutes, I looked back at the place I came to three years ago. So much has happened. It seems we were all gathered together to travel through this strange tunnel, pushed, prodded and forced down it's path to come spilling out the other end totally different. Sure we still have our same personalities, but we have grown up from silly girls to young ladies, ready to take on most any nursing job offered. We are more prepared for life too. Off came our rose-colored glasses. We can see plainly now. The world is filled with messy stuff and in some small ways we should be able to make things a little better. We are trained and ready for battle.

All the goodbyes are difficult. Some of us will work together at Wayside. Others, it may be many years or never that we see each other again in this world. Living through thick and thin for three years, we became like sisters. Remembering is strange, the bad times stick in our minds but the good times and laughter take first place. How green and innocent we were. I know there are many lessons ahead and also many memories to make. This was really a short time compared to a lifetime, but all that happened here has stamped lasting impressions on us for the rest of our lives. I am sure of it.

Everything is packed and dad is driving away. Turning my head, I take a last look. The Nurses' Home is getting smaller, fading from view – now it's gone.

Goodbye, goodbye, a bittersweet moment.

Chapter 51
State Boards
Jo Jo

The class of 1959 is now converging on our state's largest city to take the tests of all tests, the State Board Examination to receive our Registered Nurses License, a RN after our names! Sounds wonderful, Josephine Walker, RN! Some of the girls have their drivers license and are driving their parent's cars and we are pooling together. We will be staying overnight at a big hotel and the exam will be held in a very large conference room at the same hotel.

I have never stayed at a hotel before. However, the thrill of that is dampened by the anxiety I feel over the boards. Could it be after three years of study and grinding work that I might fail? We can repeat any of the failed sections twice, but after that, special classes must be taken, so the pressure is on. We were told to go over all our achievement tests, get lots of sleep (sure!) and I will add to that, say many prayers in preparation. My mind is jumping from one thing to another. They change the test every year so it's not possible to get an idea of what their emphasis might be this year. Will I even remember anything or will my mind just go completely blank?

After arriving at the hotel we went to our assigned rooms, unpacked and went to eat dinner. I haven't eaten at a big restaurant like this before. Even if it were the Ritz it wouldn't matter. I can hardly put the fork to my mouth. My stomach is saying "no" to food.

At 8 a.m. the next morning, after a long night made up of short naps, I was seated at a table with the first test section in front of me. The large room was filled with students from all over the state. We were to fill in with pencil little circles with our answers to multiple choice questions. "Answer the ones you are sure of first and then go back and think carefully about the ones you aren't sure of," this advice was given by Mrs. Caskey at Wayside. Medical Nursing was first and I wasn't sure of the first fifteen questions! The test was asking all these questions about kidney disease. We mostly concentrated on cardiac disease. Oh dear, doom is on the horizon.

Two exams that morning (timed tests). Girls started leaving and I was only halfway through. Ten minutes to go on the first exam and most of the girls still in the room were Wayside girls. Wow, we were all struggling? How smart were those other nurses?

At lunch my table discussed some of the questions and what the correct answers might be. Sitting there in a cold sweat, I realized my answers were way off. The first bites of food were choking me and ahead was an afternoon full of more test questions that I probably will not get right.

Another sleepless night and hardly anyone slept. We finished that next morning, checked out and were homeward bound. No one looked happy, few were talking, everyone seemed depressed and now we had a four to six week wait for notification in the mail.

A large envelope means you have passed, a regular sized envelope is very bad news indeed. I didn't think I could survive a retake. I know of one nurse who never did pass and just quit trying. She worked in a doctor's office and everyone knew she really wasn't a RN. I pray that won't be me!

Working at Wayside, after a few weeks, I would come home every day and check the mail. Nothing! The days crept by on snail's feet. We phoned each other and asked, "Did you get your envelope yet?"

Finally one Saturday morning, while watching for the mail man, he stopped at our box and it looked like he put in a large envelope. Could it be my test results or just another catalog? I ran out and the envelope had my name on it. With trembling fingers I opened it. <u>I passed!</u> <u>I passed!</u> I was now finally and forever a RN. I ran to tell Mom and Dad and then raced all over the neighborhood shouting the wonderful, exciting news. Where was my uniform? I think I will put it on and wear it all weekend. The dream I had for so many years has come true!

Most of the graduating classes at Wayside have an average of ten students who don't pass the first time. Wayside is very anxious about each class' testing because its reputation depends on good results. Our class, the party class, the despair of the administration, (they thought we were hopeless) all passed but two and they only failed one section each.

So hats off (or should I say, nursing caps off) to the class of 1959. The worst were really the best after all!

THE BOARD OF NURSE EXAMINERS
EXAMINATION REPORT FOR PROFESSIONAL NURSE LICENSURE
STATE BOARD TEST POOL EXAMINATION
THIS IS YOUR OFFICIAL REPORT ON THE LICENSING EXAMINATION IN THIS
JURISDICTION

CANDIDATE IDENTIFICATION – 231
YEAR OF GRADUATION – 1959

JOSEPHINE WALKER
NATIONAL STANDARD SCORES

NURSING	MEDICAL	SURGICAL	OBSTRETIC	CHILDREN	PSYCHIATRIC
TEST SCORES	627	532	502	453	553
PASSING SCORES	350	350	350	350	350

DATE OF REPORT 11/25/59

EXAMINATION DATE – OCTOBER 27-28, 1959

PASSED
THE STATE BOARD
TEST POOL
EXAMINATION

The action of the board, indicated above, is based upon this candidate's record
and performance on this examinations, in accordance with the standards adopted
by the Board of license to practice professional nursing within this jurisdiction.

License to practice professional nursing

Epilogue

Forty six girls entered Wayside in 1956, thirty five graduated in the class of 1959.

Grace Carlson – Remained at Wayside and worked there for forty-five years in Pediatrics and on several medical-surgical wards.

Reva Flanagan – Never had a full-time nursing position. Had five pregnancies in six and one half years, resulting in four children. Volunteered for the Red Cross and served as a nurse for the Girl Scouts for many years.

Feona Hartman – Worked twelve years as an office nurse for two surgeons, fifteen years as a medical-surgical nurse at a small rural hospital, four years as a Home Health nurse.

Lindsay Hinkle – Worked at Wayside in the Pediatric unit for four years and then became a full-time mother.

Katie Hatter – Worked for sixteen years full-time and part-time in labor and delivery and five years as a psychiatric nurse.

Rachael Lucas – Worked four years as a medical/surgical nurse at Wayside, eight for a local surgeon and then became a full-time mother.

Jill Lee – Worked Pediatrics for two years, then part-time at Wayside for many years in other hospital areas, retired after ten years as a home care nurse.

Pauline Macey – Worked full-time at Wayside for forty-two years in the Pediatric unit, after retirement, she worked eight years part-time in Pediatrics.

Jo Jo Walker – Worked for approximately thirty years, emergency nursing, surgery, surgical nurse for an eye surgeon, same day surgery and as evening supervisor at Wayside.

THE END

Postlogue

During the 1970's, diploma Nursing Schools closed all over the country. Wayside Nursing School closed its doors in 1975. Nursing students would now attend Community Colleges (two year programs) or Universities earning an AA degree or a BS degree in Nursing.

The "diploma nurse" earned no degrees in the three year nursing programs. Taught by experienced doctors and nurses, she has almost vanished from the medical scene. However, there are many who would say that even though today's nurses may be better educated, no one can replace the nurses who studied at these schools. The experience gained by "hands-on nursing" has never been surpassed. They were true to their motto, "The patient is always first." The class of 1959 was truly part of the "Last of the Best."

53341394R00080

Made in the USA
Lexington, KY
30 June 2016